INTRODUCTION TO CHINESE

中国税法概论

计金标　应　涛◎编著

TAX LAW AND REGULATIONS

经济管理出版社
ECONOMY & MANAGEMENT PUBLISHING HOUSE

图书在版编目（CIP）数据

中国税法概论／计金标，应涛编著 . —北京：经济管理出版社，2022.4
ISBN 978-7-5096-8392-7

Ⅰ.①中… Ⅱ.①计… ②应… Ⅲ.①税法—概论—中国 Ⅳ.①D922.22

中国版本图书馆 CIP 数据核字（2022）第 061834 号

组稿编辑：王光艳
责任编辑：张广花
责任印制：黄章平
责任校对：王淑卿

出版发行：经济管理出版社
　　　　　（北京市海淀区北蜂窝 8 号中雅大厦 A 座 11 层　100038）
网　　址：www.E-mp.com.cn
电　　话：（010）51915602
印　　刷：北京市海淀区唐家岭福利印刷厂
经　　销：新华书店
开　　本：787mm×1092mm /16
印　　张：10
字　　数：182 千字
版　　次：2022 年 6 月第 1 版　　2022 年 6 月第 1 次印刷
书　　号：ISBN 978-7-5096-8392-7
定　　价：88.00 元

FOREWORD

Hello everyone, welcome to the course of Introduction to the Tax Law and Regulations of China. This is a very important and practical course. Through the study of this course, we will not only fully understand the general concept of China's tax law, but also get familiar with the computation of tax liability for each tax item, and master the basic process of tax-related affairs and the settlement of tax disputes. Before we start the course, I believe it is necessary to make some comments about the necessity and importance of this course. In other words, why do you learn the tax law of China?

Firstly, this course is mainly for the students specialized in business management like finance, accounting, marketing, human resources management etc. Among all the courses the economic law of China is crucial to your major study. Learning knowledge of tax law will help you master economic law. So the course of tax law is also one of the important courses in the business-related majors or disciplines. We all know that tax law is also an important part of a country's jurisprudence. Because tax is a very important instrument for the government to raise revenue and regulate economic development, learning the course of tax law will not only help you master more professional tax knowledge, but also help you understand the background and intention of the Chinese government's current reform on reduction of taxes and fees. It is very helpful for you to truly enjoy the dividend of the reform.

Secondly, after completing the studies, you may join some businesses and seek professional development in economic or trade fields, especially in companies dealing with trade with China. Whether as a white-collar or a self-employed entrepreneur, you will need to deal with taxes, that is taxes of China. When we receive income, we probably need to pay individual income tax (short for IIT) . When we engaging in the deal of real estate, we should pay deed tax (short for DT), value-added tax (VAT) and stamp tax (ST) . When we buy a car, we also need to pay vehicle purchase tax (VPT) and vehicle and vessel tax (VVT) . If we choose to start our own business, there are some more taxes we need to pay, such as VAT, enterprise income tax (EIT), stamp tax, urban maintenance and construction tax (UMCT), and even excise tax (ET), urban and township land use tax (UTLST), real estate tax (RET) or many other taxes. In addition, tax intermediaries and tax agents are increasingly becoming important service industries. The study of this course will not only open the door to taxation work for everyone of you, but also bring you more convenience in dealing with tax matters in the future.

Thirdly, in almost all societies, almost every income you earn in work is subject to individual income tax, only the income after tax is freely disposable income by yourself (also known as after-tax income). Furthermore, except for very few occasions, the price of most goods and services at the market contains taxes, and almost every member of the society is more or less bearing some taxes. Taxes run through every aspect of our lives. Learning this course of tax law will not only improve the convenience in China's daily life, but also help you to clarify the rights and obligations of taxpayers, and help you to comply with Chinese tax law actively to avoid risk of violating related laws.

Targets and contents of the course:

After completing the studying of this course, students should be able to :

1. Understand the operation and scope of the China's tax law system and its administration.

2. Explain and calculate the tax payable of current 18 taxes for their taxpayers respectively.

3. Be familar with the rules about how to resolve the tax dispute between tax authorities and taxpayers.

Main Contents:

1. Overview of fundamental concept of tax law.

2. Detailed tax articles of each tax item or tax laws.

3. Administration issues.

Catalogue

Chapter

Overview of Tax Law in China

1.1 The Concept and Role of Tax Law

1.1.1 What is Tax Law

Tax law is the legal basis for tax authorities to collect taxes and taxpayers to pay taxes. It is generally enacted by the state legislature, or the state administrative departments such as the State Council of the People's Republic of China (hereinafter referred to as the State Council), the Ministry of Finance of the People's Republic of China (hereinafter referred to as the Ministry of Finance), the State Taxation Administration of the People's Republic of China (hereinafter referred to as the State Taxation Administration) relying on the authorization of the state legislature. The government relies on the implementation of the tax law to achieve a series of goals such as raising income, regulating economic structure, and promoting social equity.

There are 18 different kinds of taxes in China, which can be divided into four categories according to their nature.

(a) Goods and services taxes, including value-added tax, excise tax, vehicle purchase tax and customs duty.

(b) Income taxes, including enterprise income tax and individual income tax.

(c) Property and behavior taxes, including land appreciation tax, real estate tax, deed tax, vehicle and vessel tax, stamp duty, urban maintenance and construction tax, tobacco tax, and vessel tonnage tax.

(d) Resources and environmental taxes, including resources tax, farmland occupation tax, urban and township land use tax, environmental tax.

1.1.2 The Role of Tax Law

In addition to raising government revenue, there still are some functions derived from the basic function of raising government revenue. Firstly, tax helps to regulate the resource distribution in the market economy and helps the government to achieve economic targets in one period. In the process of raising fiscal revenue for the government, there are some options such as what to levy? how much tax to levy? and how to levy taxes? When we make different choices, it will inevitably lead to the changes not only the distribution of national income among the government and different members of society, but also the distribution of social resources among different industries, regions and enterprises. Thus, these changes will have an important impact on not only the economic behavior of micro-subjects such as enterprises and individuals, but also the proportion and status of different industries, regions and enterprises in the national economy. Since taxation includes various fields and various links of economic operation, and provides differential treatment for different economic entities, it will provide incentive effect by measures such as whether to levy taxes, collect more or less taxes. And because the rigid characteristics of mandatory collection and non-direct return, the taxation has played a powerful regulatory role. The recent deepening VAT reform, which is characterized by expanding the scope of taxation and lowering the tax rate, has a strong tax reduction effect. By transferring more economic benefits to enterprises and individuals, it is very conducive to the steady growth of the Chinese economy and the increase of people's income.

And there is other important function of taxation derived from the basic function of raising government revenue. That is helpful in promotion of equity in the whole society. The selective taxation of certain luxury consumer goods is a tax on the taxpayer's consumption, which avoids disadvantages of double taxation on savings, thus contributing to the promotion of people's savings rate. And the tax on commodity is generally included in the sales price, which is easily accepted by consumers. On the other hand, while high-income earners need to pay a larger percentage tax based on their income, the progressive tax rates of individual income tax law allow low-income earners to pay less tax or not to pay tax. This method directly reduces the disposable income of high-income people and is very popular in countries around the world to maintain social equity and reduce the gap between the rich and the poor. For example, the laws of excise tax and individual income tax are playing an important role in improving social equity.

1.2   The Factors of Tax Law

1.2.1   Taxpayers

Taxpayers refer to the units and individuals directly subject to tax liability under the tax law, and mean who will pay the tax. In general, the first article of a tax law stipulates who are the taxpayers of one tax item.

For taxpayers, there are two basic forms or types: In simple words they are individuals and units, in more formal words they are natural person and legal person or legal entity. The tax law carries out a more detailed classification on this basis, in order to implement different tax treatments. For example, natural persons can be divided into tax resident and non-tax resident, self-employed persons and other individuals, etc. Legal persons can be divided into resident enterprises and non-resident enterprises, and can also be classified according to their ownership characteristics.

1.2.2   Taxable Object

The taxable object refers to the subject of what the tax levies on, and is an important sign that distinguishes one tax from another. For example, the taxable object of excise tax is the taxable consumer goods prescribed by the excise tax law, and the taxable object of real estate tax is the real estate for business. The taxable object is the most basic or fundamental element of tax law, because it embodies the most basic boundary of taxation and determines the basic taxation scope of a certain tax. At the same time, the names of different taxes are also determined by their taxable object, such as value-added tax, enterprise income tax, individual income tax, and so on. According to their different natures, taxable objects can be divided into four categories: turnover amount of goods and services, income, property and specific behavior, resources and environment. Therefore, taxes are accordingly divided into four categories: goods and services tax, income tax and property and behavior tax, re-

sources and environment tax, as the book just discussed above.

And there are other two concepts related to taxable object: Tax base and taxable item.

Tax base is also called the basis of tax calculation. It is the direct quantity basis for calculating the tax payable of taxable object. For example, the basic calculation method of enterprise income tax payable is the taxable income multiplied by the applicable tax rate, where the taxable income is the tax base of this tax. According to its nature, there are two basic forms: value form and physical form. Value forms include taxable income, sales income, operating income, etc., which lead to Ad valorem principle. Physical forms include area, volume, weight, and so on, which lead to quantity-based principle.

The tax items are specific taxation items stipulated in the tax law by the positive enumeration to define the specific taxation scope. All economic activities listed on are classified as taxable items, and the economic activities not listed on are classified as non-taxable items. For example, *the Excise Tax Law of the People's Republic of China* (hereinafter referred to as *the Excise Tax Law*) stipulates 15 taxable items, corresponding to 15 categories of taxable consumer goods.

1.2.3 Tax Rates

The tax rate refers to the rate of collection on taxable object. It is a measure of the tax amount. The current tax rates in China mainly include flat tax rate, progressive tax rate, fixed amount tax.

1.2.3.1 Flat Tax Rate

That is, for the same taxation object, regardless of the amount, the same rate of levy is prescribed. The flat tax rate is adopted in most taxes, such as value-added tax, urban maintenance and construction tax, enterprise income tax, etc., the flat tax rate is comparatively direct and simple. If one tax is subject to flat tax, it is easy to compute the tax amount payable, you just use the equation as follow: tax amount payable = tax base×flat tax rate. For example, the current enterprises tax adopts a fundamental flat tax rate of 25%, if one enterprise earns taxable income 15 million in 2018, its enterprise income tax payable is 1500, 000×25% = 375, 000 yuan.

1.2.3.2 Progressive Tax Rate

That is, according to the amount of taxation object, it is divided into several grades. The taxable amount of different grades is applied to different tax rates. The larger the taxable amount is, the higher the applicable tax rate is. The progressive tax rate is generally used in the income tax law, and it can fully reflect the taxation principle of more taxation on more income, less taxation on less income, so as to effectively handle the vertical equity problem of tax burden.

According to the amount of taxable income, the progressive tax rate is divided into full progressive tax rate and excess progressive tax rate. The full progressive tax rate is the tax payable equal to the total amount of taxable income multiplied by the corresponding level of tax rate. The excess progressive tax rate means that the tax payable is equal to the total amount of the taxable income of each grade multiplied by the corresponding grade tax rate respectively.

1. 2. 3. 3 Fixed Amount Tax

That is, a fixed tax amount is directly specified according to the calculation unit determined by the taxable object. The fixed amount tax is applied for urban and township land use tax law and vehicle and vessel tax law. Fixed tax rate is determined by per unit such as per square meter.

1. 3 The Tax Legislation and Tax Law System of China

1. 3. 1 Laws

The fundamental tax systems are ruled by the *Tax Laws of the People's Republic of China* (hereinafter referred to as *Tax Laws of PRC*). *Tax Laws of PRC* are formulated by the National People's Congress and its Standing Committee. At present, *Tax Laws of PRC* are composed of *Individual Income Tax Law of the People's Republic of China* (short for *Individual Income Tax Law*), *Enterprise Income Tax Law of the People's Republic of China* (short for *Enterprise Income Tax Law*), *Vehicle and Vessel Tax Law of the People's Republic of China* (short for *Vehicle and Vessel Tax Law*), *Vehicle Purchase Tax Law of the People's Re-*

public of China (short for *Vehicle Purchase Tax Law*)， *Environmental Protection Tax Law of the People's Republic of China* (short for *Environmental Protection Tax Law*)， *Tobacco Tax Law of the People's Republic of China* (short for *Tobacco Tax Law*)， *Vessel Tonnage Tax Law of the People's Republic of China* (short for *Vessel Tonnage Tax Law*)， *Farmland Occupation Tax Law of the People's Republic of China* (short for *Farmland Occupation Tax Law*) and *Law of the People's Republic of China on the Administration of Tax Collection.* (short for *Tax Collection and Administration Law*)， etc.

1.3.2　Administrative Regulations and Rules

The administrative regulations and rules concerning tax are formulated by the State Council in accordance with relevant laws or under the authorization of the National's People Congress and its Standing Committee. The form of administrative regulations and rules is the provisional regulation. Except for above tax laws， currently， the highest legal norms of other taxes are the Provisional Regulations. According to the Legislative Plan of NPC， the existing provisional regulations will be replaced by tax laws in the short term.

1.3.3　Departmental Rules

It refers to the specific implementation provisions of tax laws or administrative regulations. The department rules concerning tax are formulated by the ministries of State Council which are in charge of taxation， such as Ministry of Finance of the People's Republic of China， State Taxation Administration， General Administration of Customs of the People's Republic of China， and so on.

1.3.4　Local Regulations and Rules

Based on the specific conditions and actual need of the local jurisdictions， the People's Congresses and their Standing Committees at provincial level may make local regulations and rules under the condition that they are not conflict with the *Constitution of the People's Republic of China*， laws and administrative regulations.

1. 3. 5   Procedures for Tax Legislation

There are four steps of the procedures for tax legislation: legislation proposal, examination, voting and promulgation. Firstly, on the step of legislation proposal, the ministries of State Council which are in charge of taxation propose the draft of tax law and report it to the State Council. Secondly, after examined by the State Council, the draft of tax law will be submitted to the Standing Committee of the National People's Congress. And after making corresponding amendments based on the suggestions and opinions from whole society, then the draft will be submitted to the National People's Congress and its Standing Committee for voting. At last, after the National People's Congress and its Standing Committee voted, the tax law will be issued in the name of the President of the State.

1. 4   The Related Concepts of International Taxation

At present, the contacts between China and the whole world are becoming more and more frequent. As international trade, investment, and personnel exchanges become more and more, international tax issues have arisen and increased accordingly. Since there is not an overriding international law of taxation, the term "international tax law" refers to the international aspects of the income tax law of particular countries. It is generally composed with the taxation on abroad income obtained by tax residents or resident enterprises and the taxation on domestic income received by non-tax residents or non-resident enterprises. The overlapping of tax jurisdictions from different countries leads to double taxation on income from the same source. This problem is usually resolved by concluding tax treaties among the countries.

1. 4. 1   The Concept of Jurisdiction to Tax

Income may be taxable under the tax law of a country because of a nexus between that country and the activities that generated the income. According to international usage, a jurisdictional claim based on such a nexus is called "source jurisdiction". All countries imposing an income tax excise source jurisdiction, that is, they tax income arising or having its source in their country.

A country also may impose a tax on income because of a nexus between the country and the person earning the income. A jurisdictional claim over income based on a nexus between the country that makes that claim and the person who is subject to tax is called "residence jurisdiction". Person subject to the residence jurisdiction of a country are generally taxable on their worldwide income, including both domestic-source income and foreign-source income.

With few exceptions, countries that exercise residence jurisdiction do so only with respect to the income of individuals and legal entities that they consider to be residents. Thus, the term "residence jurisdiction arises". A few countries-the United States is the primary example - exercise residence jurisdiction over their citizens as well as over their residents. That is, they assert the right to impose their income tax not only on the worldwide income of their residents, but also on the worldwide income of their non-resident citizens.

When a resident of a country earns income from outside the country (foreign-source income), the claim of that country to tax the income based on its residence jurisdiction may overlap the claim of a foreign country for tax revenue based on source jurisdiction. The claim of governments for tax revenue based on residence jurisdiction also may overlap the claims of other countries based on citizenship or, in the case of so-called "dual-resident taxpayers", on the residence claims of other countries. In addition, countries with incompatible source of income rules may both tax the same income under their source jurisdictions. Unless resolved satisfactorily, the competing claims for tax revenue based on residence and source would stifle international investment and commerce. And the tax burden imposed on persons who earn income from cross-border transactions would be unfair under traditional concepts of tax equity. So, countries have adopted some measures such as tax treaty to mitigate international double taxation.

1.4.2 Double Taxation Relief and Tax Treaties

"International double taxation" has been defined as the imposition of comparable income taxes by two or more sovereign countries on the same item of income (including capital gains) of the same taxable person for the same taxable period. This juridical or legal definition of international double taxation is a very narrow one, and should be distinguished from the broader economic concept of double taxation. Under the latter definition, double taxation occurs whenever there is multiple taxation of the same items of economic income. In most contexts, however, the legal definition is more applicable than the economic definition. The reason is that the economic definition is exceedingly broad and difficult to specific with the precision needed for tax laws.

Tax treaties represent an important aspect of the international tax rules of most countries. At present, China has successively concluded the treaties for the prevention of double taxation and the prevention of tax evasion with respect to taxes on income with 110 countries or regions. In China, the treaty prevails in the event of a conflict between the provisions of domestic law and a treaty. The most important objective of bilateral tax treaties is the elimination of double taxation. Most of the substantive provisions of the typical bilateral tax treaty are directed at the achievement of this goal by three following methods, namely deduction, exemption and credit.

1. 4. 2. 1   Deduction Method

The residence country allows its taxpayers to claim a deduction for taxes, including income tax, paid to a foreign government in respect of foreign-source income.

1. 4. 2. 2   Exemption Method

The residence country provides its taxpayers with an exemption for foreign-source income.

1. 4. 2. 3   Credit Method

The residence country provides its taxpayers with a credit against taxes otherwise payable for income taxes paid to a foreign country.

For example, tax treaties limit or eliminate the source country tax on certain types of income and require residence countries to provide relief for source country taxes either by way of a foreign tax credit or an exemption for the foreign-source income. The credit method has been adopted to relief the international double taxation in tax treaties concluded between China and other countries.

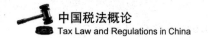

The emphasis on the elimination of double taxation should not obscure the fact that most tax treaties have another equally important objective—the prevention of fiscal evasion. Just as double taxation imposes an inappropriate barrier to international commerce, the tolerance of fiscal evasion is an explicit objective of most tax treaties.

In addition to the two principal objectives of tax treaties, there are several ancillary objectives. One is the elimination of discrimination against foreign nationals and non-residents. A second ancillary objective is the exchange of information between the contracting states. The exchange of information can be an important tool in combating fiscal evasion and may allow countries to provide taxpayers with the appropriate relief from double taxation. Finally, most contracting states provide a mechanism in their treaties for resolving disputes arising from the interaction of their tax systems.

Once a treaty has been adopted, it may be modified in minor or major ways by the mutual consent of the contracting states. It is common-place for contracting states to amend a tax treaty by entering into a protocol to the treaty. Under international law, an agreement designated as a protocol is simply a treaty under a different name. Thus, it must be ratified under the rules applicable to treaties before it becomes effective.

Chapter

Value-Added Tax (VAT) Law

Value-added tax is a kind of tax levied on the value-added amount realized in the process of commodity production and circulation or when providing labor services. Value added refers to the newly created value of workers in the process of producing goods or providing services in a certain period of time, which is the balance of the total value of goods after deducting the value transferred due to production cost.

2.1　The Characteristics of VAT

2.1.1　The General Characteristics of VAT

(1) Wide taxation scope and abundant tax sources.

(2) Implement the road link levy, but do not repeat taxation.

(3) It will not have a distorting effect on resource allocation, but has a tax neutral effect.

(4) The tax burden is passed on to the buyers along with the circulation of taxable goods, and finally borne by the final consumers of the goods.

2.1.2　Other Characteristics of China's VAT

(1) The tax is calculated outside the price, so that the indirect tax nature of VAT is more obvious.

(2) Unified implementation of the standardized purchase deduction tax law, that is, the method of deducting the tax indicated by the invoice.

(3) Taxpayers with different business scales should adopt different taxation methods.

(4) Set a number of tax rates, and set up a collection rate applicable to small-scale taxpayers.

2.2 The Scope of VAT Collection and Taxpayers

2.2.1 The Scope of VAT Collection

2.2.1.1 General Provisions on the Scope of Collection

The sale of goods, services, intangible assets or real estate within the territory of the People's Republic of China belongs to the scope of VAT collection.

2.2.1.2 Special Provisions on the Scope of Collection

(1) It is regarded as selling goods: Delivering the goods to other units or individuals for sale on a commission basis; Selling goods on a commission basis; Taxpayers with two or more institutions and unified accounting transfer goods from one institution to another for sale, except where the relevant institutions are located in the same county (city); Using the goods produced and commissioned for processing for collective welfare or individual consumption; Providing self-produced, commissioned processed or purchased goods as investment to other units or individual industrial and commercial households; Distributing the goods produced, commissioned or purchased to shareholders or investors, and giving the goods produced, commissioned or purchased to other units or individuals free of charge.

(2) Mixed sales activities: Mixed sales act refers to a sales act involving both sales of goods and provision of taxable services, which are closely connected and obtain the price from the same transferee. Sales are mixed if they involve both services and goods. Mixed sales of units and individual industrial and commercial households engaged in the production, wholesale or retail of goods shall be subject to value-added tax in accordance with the sales of goods; Other units and individual industrial and commercial households mixed sales behavior, in accordance with the sales service to pay value-added tax. The term "units and individual businesses engaged in the production, wholesale or retail of goods" as mentioned

in the book includes units and individual businesses that are mainly engaged in the production, wholesale or retail of goods and concurrently engaged in sales services.

Concurrent sales activities: The business scope of a taxpayer includes both sales of goods and taxable services, but there is no relationship between the two aspects, which does not simultaneously occur to the same purchaser or in the same sales act. Taxpayers who sell goods, provide processing and repairing services or taxable services at different tax rates or rates shall separately account for sales at different tax rates or rates. If sales are not accounted for separately, the tax rates or rates shall be applied in accordance with the following methods:

（1）For sales of goods with different tax rates, provision of processing, repair and repair services or taxable services, the higher tax rate shall apply.

（2）Sales of goods, provision of processing and repairing services or taxable services with different collection rates shall be subject to higher collection rates.

（3）For sales of goods, provision of processing and repairing services or taxable services with different tax rates and rates, the higher tax rate shall apply.

2. 2. 2　Taxpayers

2. 2. 2. 1　General Taxpayers

The taxpayers have a sound accounting and be able to accurately calculate output tax, input tax and tax payable.

2. 2. 2. 2　Small—scale Taxpayers

The taxpayers do not need to issue VAT special invoices in their operation, with their annual VAT sales of 5 million yuan or less.

When the taxpayer has a sound accounting system, even if its annual VAT taxable sales does not exceed 5 million yuan, it can also be recognized as a general taxpayer.

2.3 The Tax Rates, Tax Base and Tax Payable Calculation

2.3.1 VAT Rate

From the practice of value-added tax in various countries, the general principle to be followed when determining the value-added tax rate is to reduce the tax rate as much as possible. General provisions of vat rate in China:

(1) 13% basic tax rate.

(2) Low tax rates of 9% and 6%.

(3) Zero tax rate, applicable to export goods.

(4) Levy rate: The collection rate applicable to small-scale taxpayers shall be uniformly levied at the rate of 3%.

Table 2-1　Tax Rates of VAT

Serial Number	Tax Items	Tax Rate (%)
1	Selling or importing goods (except items 9-12)	13
2	Processing, repair and replacement services	13
3	Tangible movable property leasing service	13
4	Real estate leasing service	9
5	Selling real estate	9
6	Construction services	9
7	Transport services	9
8	Transfer of land use rights	9
9	Feed, chemical fertilizer, pesticide, agricultural machinery, agricultural film	9
10	Agricultural products such as grain, edible vegetable oil and edible salt	9
11	Tap water, heating, air conditioning, hot water, coal gas, liquefied petroleum gas, natural gas, dimethyl ether, biogas, coal products for residential use	9
12	Books, newspapers, magazines, audio-visual products and electronic publications	9

Serial Number	Tax Items	Tax Rate (%)
13	Postal service	9
14	Basic telecommunication service	9
15	Value-added telecommunications services	6
16	Financial services	6
17	Modern service	6
18	Life service	6
19	Sales of intangible assets (except land use rights)	6
20	Outward cargo	0
21	Cross-border sales of services and intangible assets within the scope prescribed by the State Council	0

Data source: The data is summarized from the *Tax Law* (2021) textbook for the Chinese CPA Examination Organized by the Chinese Institute of Certified Public Accountants (CICPA).

2.3.2   The Tax Base of VAT

The tax base of value-added tax in China is the sales of value-added tax obtained by units and individuals who sell goods or provide processing, repair and replacement services and taxable services in China, referred to as taxable sales for short.

(1) The basic provisions of taxable sales. Taxable sales of value-added tax refers to the total price collected by the taxpayer from the purchaser for selling goods or taxable services, and all the extra-price expenses collected beyond the price.

Extra-price expenses include fees, subsidies, funds, collection fees, return profits, incentive fees, liquidated damages, late payment fees, deferred payment interest, compensation, collection money, advance payment, packaging fees, packaging rent, reserve fees, quality fees, transportation handling fees and other extra-price charges of various natures.

(2) Special provisions on taxable sales. If general taxpayers sell goods or taxable services with combined pricing of sales and output tax, and small-scale taxpayers sell goods or provide taxable services with combined pricing of sales and output tax, the sales including tax shall be converted into sales excluding tax:

$$\text{Sales Amount} = \text{Sales Amount Including Tax} / (1 + \text{VAT Rate}) \qquad (2\text{-}1)$$

（3）If the price of goods or taxable services sold by taxpayers is obviously low without justifiable reasons, or if it is regarded as selling goods without sales, the sales shall be determined in the following order: ① According to the average sales price of similar goods in the recent period of taxpayers; ② According to the average sales price of similar goods of other taxpayers in the recent period; ③ According to the composition of taxable value. The formula of taxable value is:

$$\text{Composition Taxable Value} = \text{Cost} \times (1 + \text{Cost Profit Rate}) \qquad (2\text{-}2)$$

For goods subject to consumption tax, the consumption tax shall be added to the constituent taxable value.

$$\text{Composition Taxable Value} = \text{Cost} \times (1 + \text{Cost Profit Rate}) + \text{Consumption Tax}$$
$$(2\text{-}3)$$

The cost in the formula refers to the actual production cost for selling self-produced goods and the actual purchase cost for selling purchased goods. The cost profit rate in the formula is determined by the State Administration of Taxation.

• Example 2-1

In July 2019, the publishing house sold books to its independent accounting bookstore, which was settled at 35% discount. The enterprise issued a special VAT invoice indicating that the sales amount was 500, 000 yuan and the VAT amount was 45, 000 yuan. The cost of this batch of books is 520, 000 yuan.

On September 12th, the tax authorities thought that the sales price of this batch of goods was obviously low during tax inspection, so the output tax should be determined according to the composition taxable value, and the cost profit rate was 10%. Then:

$$\text{Composition Taxable Value} = \text{Cost} \times (1 + \text{Cost Profit Rate})$$
$$= 520, 000 \times (1 + 10\%)$$
$$= 572, 000 \text{ yuan} \qquad (2\text{-}4)$$
$$\text{Output Tax} = 572, 000 \times 9\%$$
$$= 51, 480 \text{ yuan} \qquad (2\text{-}5)$$

The publishing house shall pay value-added tax on the sales of the goods as follows:

$$6, 480 \text{ yuan} = 51, 480 - 45, 000 \qquad (2\text{-}6)$$

2.3.3   Calculation of the Amount of VAT Payable

Chinese current VAT levy method is the purchase deduction tax law (except for small-scale taxpayers and taxpayers of imported goods), that is, the tax is deducted according to the tax indicated on the special VAT invoice, and the difference between the output tax and the input tax is the taxable amount. Input tax means that when buying goods or taxable services, units and individuals not only pay the price of the purchased goods or taxable services themselves, but also pay the taxes borne by the goods or taxable services.

The relevant calculations are as follows:

(1) Calculation of current tax payable of general taxpayers:

Taxable Amount = Current Output Tax Amount − Current Input Tax Amount

$$(2-7)$$

(2) Calculation of tax payable of small-scale taxpayers:

Taxable Amount = Taxable Sales × Collection Rate $(2-8)$

(3) Calculation of taxable amount of imported goods. Taxable amount of imported goods, whether the taxpayer is a general taxpayer or a small-scale taxpayer, is calculated according to the composition taxable value of imported goods and the prescribed tax rate, and no input tax can be deducted. Composition of imported goods: The total amount paid by taxable value for imported goods (but excluding VAT paid) depends on whether the imported goods pay consumption tax at the same time.

1) If the imported goods are subject to consumption tax at the same time, the taxable value is:

Composition Taxable Value = Customs Duty-paid Price + Customs Duty + Consumption Tax

$$(2-9)$$

2) If the imported goods do not pay consumption tax at the same time, the composition of taxable value is:

Composition Taxable Value = Customs Duty Value + Customs Duty $(2-10)$

3) Taxable Amount = Constituent Taxable Value × Applicable Tax Rate.

* **Example   2-2**

A city post office is ageneral taxpayer of value-added tax. In July 2019, the postal universal service was provided in accordance with the country's regulations, and the postal service income tax totaled 2.9 million yuan; In accordance with the provisions of the State to provide special service business, service income tax totaled 3 million yuan. Providing other postal services, and obtaining service income and tax totaling 1.09 million yuan; Providing collection and distribution services, and obtaining service income, including tax, totaling 1.06 million yuan. It is known that the post office has obtained a total of 300,000 yuan of VAT input tax that meets the deduction conditions in the current month, but it is impossible to accurately divide the tax-exempt input tax.

How should the post office declare and pay VAT in July?

$$\text{Tax-free Income}: 290+300=590(\text{ten thousand yuan}) \tag{2-11}$$

$$\text{Total Taxable Income Tax}: 109+106=215(\text{ten thousand yuan}) \tag{2-12}$$

$$\text{Taxable Income (excluding tax)}: 109\div1.09+106\div1.06=200 \text{ (ten thousand yuan)} \tag{2-13}$$

$$\text{Transfer-out of Input Tax}: 30\times[590\div(590+200)]\approx22.41 \text{ (ten thousand yuan)} \tag{2-14}$$

$$\text{VAT Should be Declared and Paid}: (100\times9\%)+(100\times6\%)-(30-22.41)\times1.1$$
$$=6.65 \text{ (ten thousand yuan)} \tag{2-15}$$

The VAT exemption income should be declared as 5.9 million yuan.

2.4   Tax Incentive

2.4.1 VAT Reduction and Exemption

Chinese current VAT exemption items are:

(1) Self-produced agricultural products sold by agricultural producers.

(2) Contraceptive drugs and appliances.

(3) Old books.

(4) Imported instruments and equipment directly used for scientific research, scientific experiments and teaching.

（5）Imported materials and equipment aided by foreign governments and international organizations without compensation.

（6）Direct import of articles for disabled persons by organizations of disabled persons.

（7）Sales of self-used items.

In addition to the above provisions, the items of tax exemption and reduction of value-added tax shall be stipulated by the State Council, and no region or department shall stipulate the items of tax exemption and reduction. Small-scale VAT taxpayers with monthly sales below 100, 000 yuan（inclusive）are exempt from VAT.

2.4.2　Tax Refund for Export Goods with VAT

（1）Applicable scope of tax refund for export goods. Export goods that can be tax refunded（exempted）should generally meet the following four conditions：①Goods must be within the scope of value-added tax and consumption tax；②The goods must be declared for departure；③Goods that must be sold financially；④The goods must be exported and have been written off.

（2）Tax rebate rate for export goods. Chinese current export tax rebate rate is 13%, 9%, 5%, etc.

（3）Calculation method of export tax rebate. ①No levy, no refund；②To advance and retreat（advance and retreat）；③ "Exemption, offset and refund" method.

● **Example 2-3**

A general taxpayer of value-added tax who exports goods by himself has a tax rate of 13% and a tax refund rate of 10%. A batch of materials was purchased in one month, and the price indicated in the special VAT invoice was 4 million yuan. The sales of domestic goods this month is 1.2 million yuan；The sales volume of export goods is 2 million yuan（all excluding tax）. Calculate the current "exemption, credit and refund" tax amount.

（1）The current tax exemption and tax refund shall not be exempted or deducted = 200（export）×（13%−10%）= 60（ten thousand yuan）.

（2）Current tax payable = 120（domestic sales）×13%−[400（original）×13%−6] = 15.6−46 = −30.4（ten thousand yuan）.

（3）Tax amount of "exemption, offset and refund" for export goods = 200（export）× 10% = 20（ten thousand yuan）<30. 4（ten thousand yuan）

Therefore, the current tax refund amount is 200, 000 yuan.

（4）Current tax allowance = 20－20 = 0 yuan

（5）Carry－over tax deduction in the next period = 30. 4－20 = 10. 4（ten thousand yuan）.

2.5　Administration of VAT

2.5.1　The Declaration and Payment of VAT

When the VAT tax obligation occurs:

（1）The sale of goods or taxable services is the day on which the sales proceeds are received or the evidence for obtaining the sales proceeds is obtained; Where invoices are issued first, they shall be issued on the same day. The settlement method based on sales can be specifically determined as follows: ① If the goods are sold by direct collection, regardless of whether the goods are delivered or not, the date on which the sales amount is received or the proof of demand for sales amount is obtained and the bill of lading is delivered to the buyer. ②If the goods are sold by collection and acceptance and by bank collection, the day on which the goods are sent and the collection formalities are completed. ③If the goods are sold on credit or by installments, the date of collection as agreed in the contract. ④If the goods are sold by way of prepayment, the date on which the goods are dispatched. ⑤To entrust other taxpayers to sell goods on a commission basis, which is the day on which the consignment list of the consignment unit is received. ⑥For the sale of taxable services, the date on which the services are provided and the sales amount is received or the evidence of sales amount requested is obtained. ⑦Where a taxpayer acts as if he were selling goods, it shall be the day when the goods are transferred for use.

（2）The imported goods are the day when the import is declared. Special provisions in the time when the tax obligation occurs: Construction services and leasing services are provided by way of prepayment. Where a taxpayer provides construction services or lease services by way of advance payment, the time of occurrence of the tax obligation shall be the day on which the advance payment is received.

（3）The term of tax is as follows. The VAT tax period is 1 day, 3 days, 5 days, 10 days, 15 days, 1 month or 1 quarter respectively. The time limit for taxpayers to pay taxes is determined by the tax collection authority under the State Administration of Taxation in charge of value—added tax according to the amount of taxpayers' tax payable. If the tax cannot be paid for a fixed period, the tax may be paid on a case—by—case basis.

If the taxpayer pays tax in one installment of one month or one quarter, the tax shall be reported and paid within 15 days from the date of expiry. If the tax is paid on the 1st, 3rd, 5th, 10th or 15th, the tax shall be paid in advance within 5 days from the expiry date, and the tax shall be reported and paid within 15 days from the 1st of the following month and the tax payable of the previous month shall be settled.

（4）Tax location is as follows.

1）Fixed business households shall report and pay taxes to the competent tax authority in the place where their institutions are located. Where the head office and branches are not located in the same county（city）, they shall report and pay taxes to the competent tax authorities in their respective locations. Approved by the financial and taxation authority under the State Council or its authorized financial and taxation authority, the head office may report and pay taxes to the local competent taxation authority where the head office is located.

2）Fixed business households that sell goods or taxable services to other counties（cities）shall apply to the local competent tax authorities for issuing a tax administration certificate for their business activities, and report and pay taxes to the local competent tax authorities. If no certificate has been issued, it shall report and pay taxes to the competent tax authority in the place of sale or the place where the labor service occurs. Where the tax is not reported to the competent tax authority in the place where the sales or labor services are made, the competent tax authority in the place where the agency is located shall make up the tax.

3）Non—fixed business households selling goods or taxable services shall report and pay taxes to the competent tax authorities in the place where the sales or services take place. Where the tax is not reported to the competent tax authority at the place of sale or the place where the labor service occurs, the competent tax authority at the place where the

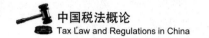

agency is located or at the place of residence shall make up the tax.

4) Imported goods shall be declared and taxed at the customs of the place where they are declared.

5) The withholding agent shall report and pay the tax withheld to the competent tax authority at the place where the withholding agent is located or at the place of residence.

2.5.2　Management of VAT Invoices

(1) The scope of use of special invoices. The collection, purchase and use of special invoices for value-added tax are limited to ordinary value-added tax payers. Small-scale taxpayers and non-value-added tax payers are not allowed to collect, purchase and use these invoices.

(2) Issuance of special VAT invoices. General taxpayers selling goods (including goods entrusted for sale), taxable services, and non-taxable services that are subject to value-added tax in accordance with the provisions of the tax law must issue special invoices for value-added tax to the purchasers or recipients.

(3) Handling of return or sales discount after issuance of special invoices. ①If the purchaser fails to pay and make accounting treatment, the purchaser must return the original invoice and tax deduction to the seller on its own initiative. ②If the purchaser has paid, or the payment for goods has not been paid but accounts have been processed, the purchaser cannot return the invoice copy and tax deduction copy to the seller, and the purchaser must obtain the purchase withdrawal or discount certificate (hereinafter referred to as the certificate) issued by the local tax authority and send it to the seller as the legal basis for issuing the scarlet letter special invoice.

Chapter

Law of Other Goods and Services Taxes

3.1　Law of Excise Tax

Excise tax is a tax levied on the turnover of specific consumer goods and consumption behavior.

There are some basic characteristics of excise tax: Firstly, the scope of excise tax is selective and flexible. Secondly, the scope of excise tax is clearly reflected the country's award-limited policy to ban from collecting. Thirdly, excise tax has a strong financial function. It can provide a steady increase in tax revenue.

3.1.1　Taxpayers of Excise Tax

Taxpayers of excise tax are units and individuals engaged in the production, processing and import of taxable consumer goods within the territory of the People's Republic of China, and other units and individuals designated by the State Council to sell taxable consumer goods.

3.1.2　The Scope of Collection

The scope of excise tax collection is the production, commissioned processing and import and sale of taxable consumer goods within the territory of the People's Republic of China.

(1) Production of taxable consumer goods.

(2) Commissioned processing of taxable consumer goods.

(3) Imports of taxable consumer goods.

(4) Retail taxable consumer goods.

(5) Specific ad valorem tax has been imposed on cigarette wholesale.

Specifically including:

(1) Over-consumption of specific consumer goods that will cause harm to human health, social order and ecological environment, such as smoke, wine, firecrackers and fireworks.

（2）Luxury goods that are not necessities of life, such as cosmetics, precious jewelry and jade.

（3）High energy consumption and high-end consumer goods, such as motorcycles, cars, yachts, etc.

（4）Non-renewable and irreplaceable scarce resources consumer goods, such as refined oil.

（5）Some consumer goods that have a broad tax base, are widely consumed, do not affect the basic livelihood of the residents after taxation and have certain financial significance.

3. 1. 3　Tax Items and Tax Rates

3. 1. 3. 1　General Provisions Applicable to Excise Tax Rates

The current excise tax takes the form of proportional tax rate and fixed tax rate.

3. 1. 3. 1. 1　Proportional Tax Rates

Taxable consumer goods subject to the proportional tax rate include tobacco, wine (except for yellow wine and beer), cosmetics, firecrackers and fireworks, precious jewelry, motorcycles, cars, golf balls and golf equipment, high-end watches, yachts, wooden disposable chopsticks and solid wood flooring, batteries, paints and other taxable items.

3. 1. 3. 1. 2　Fixed Tax Rates

Taxable consumer goods for which fixed tax rates are applicable include the sub-items of yellow wine and beer in the tax items of refined oil and wine.

3. 1. 3. 1. 3　Proportional Tax Rate Plus Fixed Tax Rate

Taxable consumer goods for which the proportional tax rate plus the fixed tax rate is applicable are cigarettes and liquor.

3. 1. 3. 2　Special Provisions on the Application of Excise Tax Rates

Where a taxpayer concurrently operates (produces and sells) taxable consumer goods with two or more tax rates, the sales volume and sales volume of the taxable consumer goods with different tax rates shall be accounted for separately. If the sales amount and sales volume are not accounted for separately or taxable consumer goods with different tax rates are sold as complete sets of consumer goods, the higher applicable tax rate shall apply.

Table 3-1   Tax Rates of Excise Tax

Taxable Items	Tax Rates
1. Tobacco	
(1) Cigarette	56%+0. 003yuan/piece
a. Class A cigarette (Production or importation)	36%+0. 003 yuan/piece
b. Class B cigarette (Production or importation)	11%+0. 005 yuan/piece
c. Wholesale (both of class A and class B)	36%
(2) Cigars	30%
(3) Cut tobacco	
2. Alcoholic drinks	
(1) White sprite	20%+0. 5 yuan per 500 milliliters
(2) Yellow wine	240 yuan per ton
(3) Beer	250 yuan per ton
a. Class A beer	220 yuan per ton
b. Class B beer	10%
(4) Other alcoholic drinks	
3. Refined oil	
(1) Gasoline	1. 52 yuan/liter
(2) Diesel oil	1. 2 yuan/liter
(3) Naphtha	1. 52 yuan/liter
(4) Solvent naphtha	1. 52 yuan/liter
(5) Lubricating oil	1. 2 yuan/liter
(6) Aviation kerosene	1. 2 yuan/liter
4. High-class cosmetics	15%
5. Precious jewelry	5%—gold, silver and platinum jewelry, diamond jewelry 10%—other jewelry, pearls, precious jade and stone
6. Firecrackers and fireworks	15%
7. Motor cars	1%-40%, determined by the cylinder capacity
8. Motor-cycles	3%—cylinder capacity less than 250ml 10%—cylinder capacity over 250ml
9. Golf and tools	10%
10. High-class watches	20%
11. Yachts	10%
12. Wood chopsticks for use only once	5%
13. Wood floor	5%
14. Batteries	4%
15. Coatings	4%

3. 1. 3. 3 Calculation of Taxable Basis and Taxable Amount of Excise Tax

3. 1. 3. 3. 1 The tax basis of Excise Tax

The current Excise Tax adopts ad valorem fixed rate and ad valorem fixed rate, and its tax basis is correspondingly divided into taxable sales amount and taxable sales amount.

(1) Ad valorem rate: Tax Payable = Sales × Proportional Tax Rate.

(2) Dependent Volume Quota: Taxable Amount = Sales Quantity × Fixed Tax Rate.

(3) Composite collection: Tax Payable = Sales Amount × Proportional Tax Rate + Sales Amount × Fixed Tax Rate.

The general provision of taxable sales, taxable sales, refers to the taxpayers selling taxable consumer goods to the buyer to collect all the price and price, but does not include the value-added tax payable to the buyer.

Special Provisions:

(1) Determination of sales amount of self-produced and self-used taxable consumer goods; Taxable consumer goods produced for own use are taxed at the selling price of the same type of consumer goods produced by the taxpayer; If there is no sales price of similar consumer goods, the tax shall be calculated based on the constituent taxable value.

(2) Taxable consumer goods commissioned for processing; Taxable consumer goods commissioned for processing are taxed at the selling price of the same consumer goods of the consignee; If there is no sales price of similar consumer goods, the tax shall be calculated based on the constituent taxable value.

(3) Imported taxable consumer goods; Taxable consumer goods imported are taxed at the constituent taxable value.

The taxable sales volume refers to the volume of taxable consumer goods. The following points should be paid attention to in determining the taxable sales volume:

(1) The sales of taxable consumer goods are the sales volume of taxable consumer goods;

(2) For self-produced taxable consumer goods for own use, the quantity transferred for use of the taxable consumer goods;

(3) Where the processing of taxable consumer goods is entrusted, the amount of taxable consumer goods recovered by the taxpayer;

(4) Where taxable consumer goods are imported, the taxable consumer goods import

tax amount approved by the customs.

3.1.3.3.2　The Calculation of the Taxable Amount of Excise Tax

The excise tax shall be subject to ad valorem fixed rate, ad valorem fixed rate, or compound tax of ad valorem fixed rate and ad valorem fixed rate.

(1) Calculation of taxable amount at ad hoc rate:

1) Taxable amount of taxable consumer goods produced and sold:

$$Taxable\ Amount = Sales \times Proportional\ Tax\ Rate \tag{3-1}$$

2) Taxable amount of self-produced, commissioned processed and imported taxable consumer goods:

$$Taxable\ Amount = Constituent\ Taxable\ Value \times Proportional\ Tax\ Rate \tag{3-2}$$

3) Taxable amount of taxable consumer goods continuously processed from purchased or commissioned processed taxable consumer goods:

$$Tax\ Payable = Sales \times Tax\ Rate - The\ Amount\ of\ Tax\ Already\ Paid$$
$$That\ is\ Deductible\ for\ the\ Current\ Period \tag{3-3}$$

(2) Calculation of taxable amount from quantity quota:

$$Taxable\ Amount = Sales\ Volume \times Fixed\ Tax\ Rate \tag{3-4}$$

(3) Calculation of taxable amount of compound tax:

$$Tax\ Payable = Sales \times Proportional\ Tax\ Rate + Sales\ Volume \times Fixed\ Tax\ Rate$$
$$\tag{3-5}$$

● **Example　3-1**

Enterprise A is a general VAT taxpayer. The following operations occurred in July:

Purchased a batch of Pu materials, the value-added tax special invoice indicated the price of 100, 000 yuan and the value-added tax of 13, 000 yuan, entrusted Enterprise B to process them into 100 golf bags, and paid 20, 000 yuan of processing fee and 26, 000 yuan of value-added tax; The sales price excluding tax for the same kind of ball bags sold by Enterprise B in the current month is RMB25, 000/bag.

For the purchase of a batch of carbon materials and titanium alloys, the special VAT invoice indicates the price of 1. 5 million yuan and VAT tax of 195, 000 yuan, and Enterprise C is entrusted to process them into golf clubs, paying processing expenses of 300, 000 yuan and VAT tax of 39, 000 yuan.

80% of the golf clubs recovered from the entrusted processing have been sold in the current month, and 3 million yuan excluding tax has been received, with 20% remaining in the warehouse.

The competent tax authority found during the tax inspection of Enterprise A in August that Enterprise B had fulfilled its obligation to collect and remit the excise tax, and Enterprise C had not fulfilled its obligation to collect and remit the excise tax.

Questions are as follows:

(1) Calculate the excise tax collected and remitted by Enterprise B.

(2) Calculate the excise tax payable by Enterprise A for sales of golf clubs.

(3) Calculate the excise tax payable on golf clubs retained by Enterprise A in the entrusted processing.

(4) Calculate the VAT payable by Enterprise A in the current month.

(5) How should the competent tax authorities deal with the failure of Enterprise C to collect and remit excise tax?

Answers are as follows.

(1) The excise tax collected and remitted by Enterprise B = $0.25 \times 100 \times 10\% = 2.5$ (ten thousand yuan).

(2) The excise tax payable by Enterprise A for sales of golf clubs = $300 \times 10\% = 30$ (ten thousand yuan).

(3) The excise tax payable on golf clubs retained in the warehouse of Enterprise A = $(150+30) \div (1-10\%) \times 10\% \times 20\% = 4$ (ten thousand yuan).

(4) Deductible input tax = $1.3 + 0.26 + 19.5 + 3.9 = 24.96$ (ten thousand yuan); Output tax = $300 \times 13\% = 39$ (ten thousand yuan); Vat payable = $39 - 24.96 = 14.04$ (ten thousand yuan).

(5) In the course of tax inspection on the entrusting party, if it is found that the entrusted party of the taxable consumer goods entrusted by the entrusting party has not collected and remitted the tax, the entrusting party shall pay the tax in arrears (the entrusted party shall not be subject to repeated tax collection, but shall be subject to a fine of more than 50% but less than 3 times the tax payable collected and remitted in accordance with the provisions of the *Law of the People's Republic of China on the Administration of Tax Collection*).

3.1.4 Tax Incentive

According to the current excise tax system in our country, unless otherwise stipulated by the State Council, excise tax is only exempted for taxable consumer goods exported. The measures for tax exemption for taxable consumer goods exported shall be formulated by the State Taxation Administration.

The exemption of taxable consumer goods for export means that the production enterprises are exempted from the excise tax in the production link according to the actual quantity of taxable consumer goods exported.

The preferential policy is only applicable to the self-operated export of the production enterprises with the right to export, or the production enterprises entrust the foreign trade enterprises to export the self-produced taxable consumer goods.

3.1.5 Administration of Excise Tax

3.1.5.1 The Production and Sale of Taxable Consumer Goods Tax Obligations Occurred

(1) Where taxable consumer goods are sold on credit and collected by instalments, the time of occurrence of the tax obligation is the date of collection stipulated in the sales contract. If the written contract does not stipulate the date of collection or there is no written contract, it is the date on which the taxable consumer goods are issued.

(2) Where taxable consumer goods are sold by way of advance receipts, the time of occurrence of the tax obligation is the day on which the taxable consumer goods are issued.

(3) Where taxable consumer goods are sold by collection acceptance and bank collection, the time of occurrence of the tax obligation is the day when the taxable consumer goods are issued and the collection procedures are completed.

(4) Where taxable consumer goods are sold by other means of settlement, the time when the tax obligation arises is the day on which the sales proceeds are received or the evidence for obtaining the sales proceeds is obtained.

3.1.5.2 The Time When the Tax Liability for Other Taxable Acts Occurs

(1) Taxable consumer goods produced by taxpayers for their own use, the time when the tax obligation occurs is the day when the taxable consumer goods are transferred for use.

(2) Where the taxpayer entrusts the processing of taxable consumer goods, the time when the tax obligation occurs is the day when the taxpayer picks up the goods.

(3) For taxable consumer goods imported by taxpayers, the time when the tax obligation arises is the day when the import is declared.

3. 1. 5. 3　Tax Period for Excise Tax

The excise tax is payable on the 1day, 3days, 5days, 10days, 15days, 1 month or 1 quarter respectively. The specific tax payment period of the taxpayer shall be separately approved by the competent tax authority according to the amount of tax payable by the taxpayer. If the tax cannot be paid for a fixed period, the tax may be paid on a case-by-case basis.

If the taxpayer takes one month or one quarter as one tax payment period, the tax shall be reported and paid within 15 days from the date of expiry. If the tax period is 1 day, 3 days, 5 days, 10 days or 15 days, the tax shall be paid in advance within 5 days from the expiry date, and the tax shall be reported and settled within 15 days from the 1st of the following month.

Taxpayers importing taxable consumer goods shall pay taxes within 15 days from the date when the customs issues the special payment letter for customs import excise tax.

3. 1. 5. 4　Tax Location for Excise Tax

(1) Taxable consumer goods sold by taxpayers, as well as self-produced and self-used taxable consumer goods, unless otherwise stipulated by the financial and tax authorities under the State Council, shall report and pay taxes to the competent tax authorities at the place where the taxpayer's organization is located or at the place of residence.

(2) Taxable consumer goods commissioned for processing, except for those for which the trustee is an individual, shall be paid excise tax by the trustee to the competent tax authority at the place where the institution is located or at the place of residence. Taxable consumer goods commissioned to be processed by individuals shall be reported and taxed by the entrusting party to the competent tax authority at the place where the agency is located or at the place of residence.

(3) Imported taxable consumer goods shall be declared and taxed by the importer or his agent to the customs at the place of declaration.

(4) Taxpayers who sell or entrust other counties (cities) to sell self-produced taxable consumer goods, after the sales of taxable consumer goods, report and pay taxes to the competent tax authority at the place where the agency is located or at the place of residence.

(5) If the head office and branches of the taxpayer are not located in the same county

(city), they shall report and pay taxes to the competent tax authorities in the places where their respective offices are located; Approved by the Ministry of Finance, the State Taxation Administration or its authorized financial and tax authorities, the head office may report and pay taxes to the competent tax authority in the place where the head office is located.

(6) Taxable consumer goods sold by taxpayers, if returned by the purchaser for reasons such as quality, may be refunded the excise tax already paid upon examination and approval by the competent tax authority in the place where the agency is located or the place of residence.

3.2　Urban Maintenance and Construction Tax Law

3.2.1　Scope of Taxation

UMCT is levied on units and individuals engaged in industrial and commercial operations that pay value-added tax and excise tax. It has the following characteristics:

Firstly, the tax is earmarked for the maintenance and construction of urban public utilities and public facilities.

Secondly, it belongs to a kind of additional tax, and the urban construction tax itself has no specific and independent tax object, and its collection and management method is also completely handled according to the relevant provisions of the "two taxes".

Thirdly, different proportional tax burden levels are designed according to the size of the cities and towns where the taxpayers are located and the capital needs. According to the location of taxpayers, there are three grades, namely 7%, 5% and 1%.

Fourthly, the tax scope of UMCT is relatively wide. In view of the fact that value-added tax and excise tax are the main taxes in the current tax system of our country and urban maintenance and construction tax is its additional tax, in principle, the scope of taxpayers of urban maintenance and construction tax covers the scope of taxpayers of value-add-

ed tax and excise tax, so the scope of collection is relatively wide.

3.2.2 Taxpayers

Taxpayers of UMCT refer to the units and individuals that are obligated to pay the "two taxes" of value-added tax and excise tax.

3.2.3 Tax Rates

(1) UMCT adopts the proportional tax rate based on regional differences. Taxpayers are located in different regions, and the applicable tax rates do not pass. The specific provisions are as shown in the table 3-2:

Table 3-2   Tax Rates of UMCT

Tax Taxpayer's Location	Tax Rate
Urban	7%
Counties and towns	5%
Not in urban areas, counties or towns	1%

(2) Exceptions. ①For the units and individuals whose taxes are withheld and collected by the trustee, the urban construction tax withheld and collected shall be implemented according to the applicable tax rate at the place where the trustee is located. ②Units and individuals without fixed tax payment places, such as mobile operation, pay "two taxes" at the place of business, and their urban construction tax shall be paid at the applicable tax rate at the place of business.

3.2.4 Tax Basis

3.2.4.1 General Provisions

(1) Taxpayers in violation of the relevant provisions of the "two taxes" and additional fines and fines, not as the basis for urban construction tax.

(2) Taxpayers who violate the relevant provisions of the "two taxes" and are investiga-

ted and compensated for the "two taxes" and are fined should also pay taxes and fines for the unpaid urban construction tax.

(3) The "two taxes" will be reduced or exempted, and the urban construction tax will be reduced or exempted at the same time.

3. 2. 4. 2   Special Provisions

UMCT is not levied on import and export. If the customs collect value-added tax and excise tax on import link, urban construction tax will not be levied along with it. And if the value-added tax and excise tax are refunded for export, the paid UMCT will not be refunded.

3. 2. 5   Calculation of Taxable Amount

Taxable amount = (Actually paid VAT+Actually paid excise tax)×Applicable tax rate

- **Example   3-2**

An enterprise located in the urban area paid a total of 5. 62 million yuan of value-added tax, excise tax and customs duties in August. Among them, the customs duty is 1. 02 million yuan, and the value-added tax and excise tax paid in the import link are 2. 6 million yuan. What is the UMCT that the enterprise should pay in August?

The UMCT payable = (562-102-260)×7% = 14(ten thousand yuan)

(3-6)

3. 3   Customs Duty Law

Customs duty (tariffs) is levied by the national customs on goods or articles entering or leaving the customs territory of country.

3. 3. 1   Taxpayers

The taxpayer is the consignee of the imported goods, the consignor of the exported

goods and the owner of the imported goods. It is also an agent entrusted to handle the import and export formalities of goods.

The taxpayer of non-trade goods is postal tax. It includes several characteristics, including the holder of the luggage and articles carried by the inbound passengers, holders of goods brought into the country by service personnel on various means of transport for their own use, the owner of the gift or other entry, consignee of imported personal mail.

3.3.2　Tax Rates

Tariff rates are divided into import tariff rates, export tax rates and provisional tax rates.

(1) Import tariff rate. Import duties are subject to MFN rates, agreed rates, preferential rates, general rates, tariff quota rates, etc.

(2) Export tax rate. Differential proportional tax rates are generally applied.

(3) Provisional tax rates. Provisional tax rates may be applied to import and export goods for a certain period of time.

3.3.3　Determination of the Origin of the Imported Goods

There are two ways to determine the origin:

(1) All production standards of origin. That is, for imported goods produced or manufactured entirely within one country, the country of production or manufacture is the country of origin of the goods.

(2) Substantive processing standards. It refers to the imported goods processed and manufactured in several countries, with the last country that economically can be regarded as the substantial processing of the goods as the country of origin of the relevant goods.

3.3.4　Tax Base of Customs Duty (Customs Value of Customs Duties)

The customs value of customs duties is the price on which customs duties are levied.

3.3.4.1　The Customs Value of the Imported Goods

The CIF value of imported goods is the customs value based on the transaction price approved by the customs.

CIF price refers to the delivery price including the price of the goods and the packing, freight, insurance and other labor costs before the goods arrive at the import place within the territory of our country. For the fees that are not included in the customs value accounting or should be deducted, the customs shall adjust the transaction price.

The following fees for imported goods shall be included in the customs value: ①Commissions and brokerage fees other than purchase commissions borne by the buyer; "Purchase Commission" refers to the labor expenses paid by the buyer to his own procurement agent for the purchase of imported goods. ② The cost borne by the buyer of the container which is considered to be integral with the goods at the time of the examination to determine the customs value. ③The cost of packaging materials and packaging services borne by the buyer. ④The price of materials, tools, moulds, consumable materials and similar goods provided by the buyer free of charge or less than the cost in relation to the production and sale of the goods to China, which may be allocated in an appropriate proportion, and the expenses of related services such as development and design abroad. ⑤The royalty that the buyer must pay in relation to the goods as a condition of their sale in China. ⑥Proceeds obtained by the seller, directly or indirectly, from the buyer from the resale, disposal or use of the goods after import.

The following taxes and fees on imported goods are not included in the customs value of the goods: ①The cost of construction, installation, assembly, maintenance and technical services after the import of plant, machinery, equipment and other goods. ②The transportation of the imported goods upon their arrival at the place of import within the territory of China and their related expenses and insurance premiums. ③ Import duties and domestic taxes.

Calculation of customs value:

$$\text{Customs Value} = \text{FOB} + \text{Freight} + \text{Insurance Fee} \qquad (3\text{--}7)$$

3. 3. 4. 2   Customs Valuation Method for Imported Goods

If the transaction value of the imported goods does not conform to the provisions of the tax law, or the transaction value cannot be determined, the customs shall assess the customs value in the following order:

(1) The transaction price of the same goods sold into China at or about the same time as the goods.

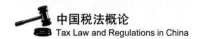

(2) The transaction price of similar goods sold into China at or about the same time as the goods.

(3) The unit price of the maximum total sales volume of the same or similar imported goods sold to unrelated buyers in the first level of sales at the same time or approximately at the same time as the import of the goods, net of the following: ①The usual profits and general expenses and the usual commissions paid when goods of the same class or class are sold in the first-level sales segment within the territory of the People's Republic of China. ②The transportation of the imported goods upon their arrival at the place of import within the territory of China and their related expenses and insurance premiums. ③Import duties and domestic taxes.

(4) Price calculated on the basis of the sum of the following: cost of materials used in the production of the goods and processing expenses, profit and general expenses normally incurred in selling goods of the same class or kind to the territory of the People's Republic of China, transportation of the goods before their arrival at the place of import within the territory and related expenses and insurance premium.

(5) Prices assessed by reasonable means.

3.3.4.3 Customs Value of Export Goods

The customs value of export goods shall be determined by the customs on the basis of the transaction value of the goods and the transportation of the goods to the place of export within the territory of the People's Republic of China before loading and the related fees and insurance premiums.

The transaction price of the exported goods refers to the total price that the seller shall receive directly and indirectly from the buyer for the export of the goods at the time of export. Export duties are not included in the customs value.

The calculation formula is:

$$\text{Customs Value} = \text{FOB} \div (1 + \text{Export Tax Rate}) \tag{3-8}$$

3.3.5   Calculation of Taxable Amount of Customs Duties

The calculation formula of taxable amount is:

$$\text{Taxable Amount} = \text{Quantity of Taxable Import and Export Goods} \times$$

Unit Customs Value×Applicable Tax Rate $\qquad$ (3-9)

- **Example 3-3**

When a company imports 100 microcomputers and converts them into RMB, the dutiable value of each microcomputer is 10, 000 yuan, the ordinary tax rate is 70%, and the preferential tax rate is 20%. The tax payable of the company is calculated.

(1) According to the formula:

Taxable Amount = Quantity of Goods Payable×Unit Customs Value×Applicable Tax Rate

(3-10)

(2) At ordinary tax rates:

$\qquad$ Tax Payable = 100×10, 000×70% = 700, 000 yuan $\qquad$ (3-11)

(3) At preferential rates:

$\qquad$ Tax Payable = 100×10, 000×20% = 200, 000 yuan $\qquad$ (3-12)

3. 4 Vehicle Acquisition Tax Law

The purchase of vehicles that have been subject to vehicle acquisition tax is no longer subject to vehicle acquisition tax.

3. 4. 1 Taxpayers

Units and individuals who purchase automobiles, trams, trailers and motorcycles with exhaust volume exceeding 150 ml (hereinafter referred to as taxable vehicles) are taxpayers of vehicle acquisition tax, and shall pay vehicle acquisition tax in accordance with the provisions of *Vehicle Acquisition Tax Law of the People's Republic of China* (hereinafter referred to as *Vehicle Acquisition Tax*).

3. 4. 2 Tax Rate

The tax rate of vehicle acquisition tax is 10%.

3.4.3　Tax Incentive

The following vehicles are exempt from vehicle acquisition tax：①Vehicles used by foreign embassies, consulates, international organizations in China and their related personnel that should be exempted from tax in accordance with the law；②Vehicles included in the equipment ordering plan of the Chinese People's Liberation Army and the Chinese People's Armed Police Force；③The national comprehensive fire rescue vehicles hanging the special number plate for emergency rescue；④Non－transportation－dedicated operation vehicles with fixed devices；⑤Public buses and trams purchased by urban public transport enterprises.

3.4.4　The Calculation of Taxable Value and Taxable Amount of Taxable Vehicles

According to the following provisions：

Firstly, the taxable value for taxpayers to purchase taxable vehicles for their own use is the total price actually paid by taxpayers to sellers, excluding VAT tax. Secondly, taxable value where taxpayers import taxable vehicles for their own use, adding customs duties and excise tax to the customs duty－paid value. Thirdly, the taxable value of taxable vehicles produced by taxpayers for their own use shall be determined according to the sales price of similar taxable vehicles produced by taxpayers, excluding VAT tax. At last, the taxable value for taxpayers to obtain taxable vehicles for their own use by giving gifts, winning prizes or other means shall be determined according to the price stated in the relevant certificates when purchasing taxable vehicles, excluding VAT tax.

(1) Taxable value. When taxpayers purchase taxable vehicles for their own use, taxable value includes the total price and extra－price expenses paid to the seller for taxpayers to purchase taxable vehicles (including handling fees, funds, liquidated damages, packaging fees, transportation fees, storage fees, collection money, advance payment and other fees charged by the seller to the buyer outside the vehicle price), but excluding VAT tax.

(2) The formula for calculating the taxable value of taxable vehicles imported by taxpayers for their own use is：

Taxable Value = Customs Duty Value+Customs Duty+Excise Tax　　(3-13)

(3) The taxable value of taxable vehicles produced, donated, awarded or obtained by other means for taxpayers' own use shall be determined by the competent tax authorities with reference to the minimum taxable value as prescribed in these regulations.

(4) In order to ensure that the tax basis is reasonable and accurate, the State Taxation Administration stipulates the minimum taxable value of different types of taxable vehicles with reference to the average transaction price of taxable vehicles in the market. Taxpayers who purchase or import taxable vehicles for their own use, whose declared taxable value is lower than the minimum taxable value of the same type of taxable vehicles, and without justifiable reasons, shall levy vehicle acquisition tax according to the minimum taxable value.

(5) If the taxpayer settles the taxable vehicle price in foreign exchange, it shall be converted into RMB to calculate the taxable amount according to the RMB benchmark exchange rate announced by the People's Bank of China on the date of tax declaration (or the exchange rate calculated according to relevant regulations).

Chapter

4

Enterprise Income Tax (EIT) Law

Enterprise income tax is levied on the production and operation income and other income of enterprises and other income organizations in China.

4.1　Taxpayers and the Scope of EIT

4.1.1　Taxpayers

The taxpayer of enterprise income tax refers to the enterprises and other income earning organizations within the territory of the People's Republic of China. Except for sole proprietorship enterprises and partnership enterprises, which are not subject to the enterprise income tax law, all enterprises and other income earning organizations (hereinafter referred to as enterprises) within the territory of China shall pay enterprise income tax in accordance with the provisions of this law.

4.1.1.1　Resident Enterprises

Resident enterprises refer to enterprises established in China according to law, or established in accordance with the laws of foreign countries (regions), but with actual management organizations in China.

4.1.1.2　Non-resident Enterprises

Non-resident enterprises are the enterprises which are established in accordance with foreign laws and whose actual management organization is not in China, but have an institution or place in China, or the enterprises that do not have an institution or place in China but have income from China.

4.1.2　Tax Object

The object of enterprise income tax refers to the enterprise's income from production

and operation, other income and liquidation income.

A resident enterprise shall tax its income from sources inside and outside China.

If a non-resident enterprise establishes an institution or place within the territory of China, it shall pay enterprise income tax on the income derived from the establishment of the institution or place in China and the income generated outside China but actually connected with its establishment.

A non-resident enterprise that does not have an establishment in China, or which have an establishment or place of business in China but whose income is not effectively connected with such an establishment or place of business shall be subject to income tax on its China-sourced income on a withholding basis.

Determination of sources of income:

(1) Income from sales of goods.

(2) Income from providing services.

(3) Income from the transfer of property.

(4) Determination of income from equity investment such as dividends.

(5) Interest income, rent income and royalty income.

(6) Other income.

4.1.3   Tax Rates

(1) The basic tax rate is 25%. It is applicable to resident enterprises and non-resident enterprises with institutions and places in China and the income is related to the institutions and fields.

(2) The low tax rate is 20%. It is applicable to non-resident enterprises that have not set up institutions or places in China, or have established institutions or places, but their income has no actual connection with the institutions or places they set up. However, the tax rate of 10% is applicable to the actual taxation.

4.2   Taxable Income

The amount of taxable income is the tax basis of enterprise income tax. According to the provisions of the *Enterprise Income Tax Law*, the amount of taxable income is the total income of the enterprise in each tax year, after deducting the non−tax income, tax−free income, various deductions and the loss of previous years allowed to be made up. The basic formula is as follows:

$$\text{Taxable Income} = \text{Total Income} - \text{Non−taxable Income} -$$
$$\text{Tax Exempt Income} - \text{Various Deductions} -$$
$$\text{Losses of Previous Years Allowed to be Made Up}$$

$$(4-1)$$

4. 2. 1 Total Revenue

The total income of an enterprise includes the income obtained from various sources in both monetary and non−monetary forms. Specifically, it includes income from sales of goods, income from providing labor services, income from transfer of property, dividend and other equity investment income, interest income, rent income, royalty income, donation acceptance income and other income.

4. 2. 2 Non−Taxable Income and Tax Free Income

4. 2. 2. 1 Non−taxable Income

(1) Financial appropriation refers to the financial funds allocated by people's governments at all levels to institutions, social organizations and other organizations incorporated into budget management.

(2) Non−taxable income also includes the administrative fees and government funds collected according to law and incorporated into financial management.

(3) Other non−taxable income as stipulated by the State Council is included.

4. 2. 2. 2 Tax Free Income

The dividends, bonuses and other equity investment income that are actually connected with the institution or establishments of non−resident enterprises set up in China. And the dividends, bonuses and other equity investment income must be obtained from the resident enterprise of China.

（1）Interest income of national debt.

（2）The equity income such as dividend and bonus between qualified resident enterprises.

（3）Income of qualified non-profit organizations.

4.2.3　Scope of Deductions

According to the *Enterprise Income Tax Law*, reasonable expenses related to the income obtained by an enterprise, including costs, expenses, taxes, losses and other expenses, are allowed to be deducted when calculating the taxable income.

Firstly, the expenditure incurred by an enterprise should be distinguished between income expenditure and capital expenditure. Income expenditure shall be directly deducted in the current period of occurrence. Capital expenditure shall be deducted by stages or included in the cost of relevant assets, and shall not be directly deducted in the current period.

Secondly, the expenses or property formed by the non-taxable income of an enterprise for expenditure shall not be deducted or the corresponding depreciation and amortization deduction shall be calculated.

Thirdly, unless otherwise stipulated in the enterprise income tax law and these regulations, the actual costs, expenses, taxes, losses and other expenses incurred by an enterprise shall not be deducted repeatedly.

4.2.3.1　Deduction Items and Their Standards

（1）Staff welfare, trade union funds, staff education funds. ①The employee welfare expenses incurred by the enterprise, which does not exceed 14% of the total wages and salaries, can be deducted. ②The trade union funds allocated by the enterprise, which does not exceed 2% of the total wages and salaries, can be deducted. ③The part of employee education expenses incurred by the enterprise, which does not exceed 8% of the total wages and salaries since January 1st, 2018, is allowed to be deducted when calculating the taxable income of enterprise income tax; the excess part is allowed to be carried forward and deducted in the following tax years.

（2）Business entertainment expenses. The business entertainment expenses related to production and operation activities of an enterprise shall be deducted according to 60% of the amount incurred, but the maximum amount shall not exceed 5 ‰ of the sales (business) income of the current year.

(3) Advertising expenses and business publicity expenses. For the qualified advertising and business publicity expenses incurred by an enterprise, the part not exceeding 15% of the sales (business) income of the current year shall be allowed to be deducted; the excess part shall be allowed to be deducted in the tax year after being carried forward.

(4) Public welfare donation expenditure. The public welfare donation expenses incurred by an enterprise, which does not exceed 12% of the total annual profits, are allowed to be deducted. The part exceeding 12% of the total annual profit is allowed to be carried forward and deducted in the calculation of taxable income within the next three years.

4.2.3.2　Items Not to be Deducted

In calculating the amount of taxable income, the following expenditures shall not be deducted:

(1) Dividends and other equity investment income paid to investors.

(2) Enterprise income tax.

(3) The tax overdue fine refers to the overdue fine imposed by the tax authorities in violation of the tax laws and regulations.

(4) The losses of fines and confiscated property refer to the fines imposed by the relevant departments in violation of the relevant laws and regulations of the State, as well as the fines and confiscated properties imposed by judicial organs.

(5) Donation expenditure exceeding the prescribed standard.

(6) Sponsorship expenditure refers to all kinds of non-advertising expenditures that have nothing to do with production and operation activities.

(7) The non-approved reserve expenditure refers to the provision for impairment of assets, risk reserve and other reserve expenses that do not conform to the provisions of the financial and tax authorities of the State Council.

(8) Management fees paid between enterprises, rents and royalties paid between business organizations in enterprises, and interest paid between business organizations in non-banking enterprises shall not be deducted.

(9) Other expenses not related to income.

4. 2. 4　Make up for Loss

The loss of an enterprise in a tax year can be made up with the income of the next year. If the income of the next year is not enough to make up, it can continue to make up year by year, but the longest period shall not exceed five years. Moreover, when an enterprise collects and calculates the enterprise income tax, the loss of its overseas business organization shall not offset the profit of its domestic business organization.

4. 3　Tax Preference

The preferential ways of enterprise income tax stipulated in the tax law include tax exemption, tax reduction, additional deduction, accelerated depreciation, reduced income, tax credit, etc.

4. 3. 1　Tax Exemption and Tax Reduction

(1) The income of an enterprise engaged in the following items shall be exempted from enterprise income tax: ①Planting of vegetables, grains, potatoes, oil, beans, cotton, hemp, sugar, fruit and nuts; ②Breeding of new crop varieties; ③The cultivation of traditional Chinese medicine; ④Cultivation and planting of trees; ⑤Raising livestock and poultry; ⑥Collection of forest products; ⑦Irrigation, primary processing of agricultural products, veterinary medicine, agricultural technology extension, agricultural machinery operation and maintenance, etc; ⑧Ocean fishing.

(2) The enterprise income tax shall be reduced by half on the income from enterprises engaged in the following items: ①Cultivation of flowers, tea and other beverage crops and spice crops; ② Mariculture, inland aquaculture; ③Income from qualified environmental protection and energy and water saving projects.

The income from environmental protection, energy conservation and water saving projects shall be exempted from enterprise income tax from the first year to the third year and reduced by half from the fourth year to the sixth year.

The income from investment and operation of public infrastructure projects supported by the State shall be exempted from enterprise income tax from the first year to the third year and reduced by half from the fourth year to the sixth year.

4. 3. 2   Preferential Treatment for High-tech Enterprises

The high-tech enterprises that need to be supported by the State shall be subject to enterprise income tax at a reduced rate of 15%.

Since January 1st, 2010, issues related to the applicable tax rate and tax credit for overseas income of high-tech enterprises shall be implemented in accordance with the following provisions:

The income from overseas sources of high-tech enterprises, which have been applied for and recognized by the total amount of research and development expenses, total income, total sales income and high-tech products（services）income related to all domestic and overseas production and operation activities, can enjoy the preferential policy of high-tech enterprise income tax, that is, the income from overseas can be paid at the preferential tax rate of 15%. For enterprise income tax, when calculating the overseas credit limit, the total amount of tax payable at home and abroad can be calculated according to the preferential tax rate of 15%.

4. 3. 3   Preferential Treatment for Advanced Technology Service Enterprises

Since January 1st, 2017, the enterprise income tax will be levied at a reduced rate of 15% for the identified technologically advanced service enterprises nationwide.

4. 3. 4   Preferential Treatment for Small and Low Profit Enterprises

Small and low profit enterprises shall be subject to enterprise income tax at a reduced rate of 20%.

4. 3. 5 Additional Deduction

Additional deduction refers to additional deduction on the basis of pretax deduction of enterprise expenditure items according to the prescribed proportion.

4. 3. 5. 1 Research and Development Expenses of Enterprises

Research and development expenses, from 2018 to December 31st, 2020, if no intangible assets are included in the current profits and losses, they shall be deducted according to 75% of the research and development expenses after deducting according to the actual situation according to the regulations; if the intangible assets are formed, they shall be amortized at 175% of the cost of the intangible assets.

4. 3. 5. 2 Overseas R&D Expenses Entrusted by Enterprises and Pretax Additional Deduction

The overseas R&D expenses entrusted by the enterprise shall be included in the entrusted overseas R&D expenses of the entrusting party according to 80% of the actual amount of the expenses. The part not exceeding 2/3 of the qualified domestic R&D expenses can be added and deducted before the enterprise income tax.

4. 3. 5. 3 Wages Paid by Enterprises for the Placement of Disabled Persons

The additional deduction of wages paid by the enterprise for the placement of disabled personnel refers to the additional deduction of 100% of the wages paid to the disabled employees on the basis of the actual deduction of the wages paid to the disabled employees.

4. 3. 6 Accelerated Depreciation Discount

If it is really necessary to accelerate the depreciation of fixed assets of an enterprise due to technical progress and other reasons, the depreciation period may be shortened or the method of accelerated depreciation may be adopted. If the method of shortening the depreciation period is adopted, the minimum depreciation period shall not be less than 60% of the prescribed depreciation period. If the accelerated depreciation method is adopted, the double declining balance method or the sum of years method may be adopted.

4.4　Calculation of Tax Payable

The income tax payable by a resident enterprise is equal to the taxable income multiplied by the applicable tax rate. The basic calculation formula is as follows:

Tax Payable＝Taxable income×Applicable Tax Rate−Tax Deduction−Tax Credit

(4-2)

There are generally two ways to calculate the amount of taxable income, namely the direct calculation method and the indirect calculation method.

4.4.1　Direct Calculation Method

Under the direct calculation method, the taxable income is the balance of the total income of the enterprise in each tax year after deducting the non−tax income, tax−free income, various deductions and the losses of previous years allowed to be made up. The basic calculation formula is as follows:

Taxable Income＝Total Income−Non−taxable Income−Tax Exempt Income−Various Deductions−Losses of previous years allowed to be Covered

(4-3)

4.4.2　Indirect Calculation Method

Under the indirect calculation method, the taxable income is the amount of taxable income after the amount of items adjusted according to the tax law is added or subtracted on the basis of the total accounting profits. The calculation formula is as follows:

Taxable Income＝Total Accounting Profit ±Amount of Tax Adjustment Items

(4-4)

The amount of tax adjustment items includes two aspects: One is the amount that should be adjusted if the scope of tax regulation is inconsistent with the accounting regulation; The other is the amount that should be adjusted if the deduction standard stipulated by tax law is inconsistent with the accounting regulation.

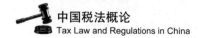

● **Example 4-1**

There is an enterprise which is a resident enterprise, and its business operations in 2019 are as follows:

(1) 40 million yuan in sales revenue.

(2) The sales cost of the products to be carried forward is 26 million yuan.

(3) There are 7.7 million yuan of sales expenses (including 6.5 million yuan of advertising expenses), 4.8 million yuan of management expenses (including 250,000 yuan of business entertainment expenses), and 600,000 yuan of financial expenses.

(4) Sales tax is 1.6 million yuan (including 1.2 million yuan of value-added tax).

(5) The non-operating income is 800,000 yuan, and the non-operating expenditure is 500,000 yuan (including 300,000 yuan donated to poor mountainous areas through public welfare social organizations, and 60,000 yuan of tax overdue fine is paid).

(6) Included in the costs and expenses, the total amount of paid wages is 2 million yuan, the allocated labor union funds are 50,000 yuan, the staff welfare expenses are 310,000 yuan, and the staff education expenses are 70,000 yuan.

Requirement: Calculate the enterprise income tax actually payable by the enterprise in 2019.

Answers:

(1) Total Accounting Profit = 4,000+80-2,600-770-480-60-40-50 = 80(ten thousand yuan)

(2) The Increase of Advertising and Business Publicity Expenses = 650-4,000×15% = 650-600 = 50(ten thousand yuan)

(3) Income from Business Entertainment Expenses Increase = 25-25×60% = 25-15 = 10(ten thousand yuan)

4,000×5 ‰ = 20(ten thousand yuan) > 25×60% = 15(ten thousand yuan)

(4) The Income of Donation Expenses Should be Increased = 30-80×12% = 20.4(ten thousand yuan)

(5) The Income of Trade Union Funds Should be Increased = 5-200×2% = 1(ten thousand yuan)

(6) The Amount of Income to be Increased in Employee Welfare Expenses = 31-200× 14% = 3(ten thousand yuan)

(7) Deduction Limit of Staff Education Funds = 200×8% = 16(ten thousand yuan)

If the actual amount is less than the deduction limit, no tax adjustment will be made.

(8) Taxable Income = 80+50+10+20. 4+6+1+3 = 170. 4(ten thousand yuan)

(9) Enterprise Income Tax Payable in 2019 = 170. 4×25% = 42. 6(ten thousand yuan)

• Example   4-2

There is an industrial enterprise which is a resident enterprise, and its business operations in 2019 are as follows:

The annual sales revenue was 56 million yuan, and the cost of product sales was 4 million yuan. They are as follows: 1. 0 million yuan of other business income, 8 million yuan of other business income and 6. 94 million yuan of other business costs; 0. 4 million yuan of interest income from the purchase of national debt; 3 million yuan of non−value−added tax sales tax and surcharges; 7. 6 million yuan of management expenses, including 600, 000 yuan of research and development expenses of new technology, 700, 000 yuan of business entertainment expenses, 2 million yuan of financial expenses, and the right of direct investment in other resident enterprises; The profit – making income is 340, 000 yuan (the income tax has been paid at the investor's location at the tax rate of 15%); The non−operating income is 1 million yuan, and the non−operating expenditure is 2. 5 million yuan (including 380, 000 yuan of public welfare donation) .

Requirement: Calculate the enterprise income tax payable by the enterprise in 2019.

Answers:

(1) Total Profit = 5, 600+800+40+34+100−4, 000−694−300−760−200−250 = 370 (ten thousand yuan).

(2) The interest income of national debt is exempt from enterprise income tax, and the income should be reduced by 400, 000 yuan.

(3) Income from Technology Development Fee Reduction = 60×75% = 45(ten thousand yuan).

(4) 60% of the Actual Business Entertainment Expenses = 70×60% = 42(ten thousand yuan).

Calculated by 5 ‰ of Sales (Business) Income = (5, 600+800)×5 ‰ = 32 (ten thousand yuan).

According to the regulations, the pretax deduction limit should be 32 ten thousand yuan, and the actual taxable income should be increased = 70−32 = 38(ten thousand yuan).

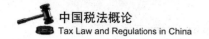

（5）The equity income obtained from direct investment in other resident enterprises belongs to tax-free income, and the taxable income shall be reduced by 340, 000 yuan.

（6）Donation Deduction Standard = 370×12% = 44. 4(ten thousand yuan).

The actual donation amount of 38 ten thousand yuan is less than the deduction standard of 44. 4 ten thousand yuan, which can be deducted according to the actual amount of donation without tax adjustment.

（7）Taxable Income = 370-40-45+38-34 = 289(ten thousand yuan).

（8）The Enterprise Income Tax Payable by the Enterprise in 2019 = 289×25% = 72. 25 (ten thousand yuan).

4.5　Administration of EIT

4.5.1　Tax Location

Unless otherwise stipulated in tax laws and administrative regulations, the tax paying place of resident enterprises shall be the place where the enterprises are registered. However, if the registration place is overseas, the place where the actual management organization is located shall be the tax paying place.

If a resident enterprise establishes a business organization without the legal person status in China, it shall calculate and pay the enterprise income tax in summary.

If a non-resident enterprise establishes an institution or place in China, the place where the institution or place is located shall be regarded as the tax paying place for the income derived from inside China by the non-resident enterprise and the income generated outside China but actually connected with the establishment or site.

If a non-resident enterprise does not have an institution or place in China, or if it has established an institution or place, but the income it obtains has no actual connection with its establishment, the place where the withholding agent is located shall be regarded as the tax paying place.

4.5.2 Tax Payment Period

Enterprise income tax is calculated and collected annually, paid monthly or quarterly, and settled at the end of the year, with more refund and less compensation.

The tax year of enterprise income tax is from January 1st to December 31st of the Gregorian calendar.

Within 5 months from the end of the year, submit the annual enterprise income tax return to the tax authorities, and settle the final settlement of the payable and refundable taxes.

4.5.3 Tax Returns

If it is paid in advance on a monthly or quarterly basis, it shall, within 15 days from the end of the month or quarter, submit to the tax authorities a tax return for prepayment of enterprise income tax.

When submitting the enterprise income tax return, the enterprise shall attach the financial accounting report and other relevant materials in accordance with the provisions.

4.5.4 Withholding Source

The income tax payable by a non-resident enterprise that does not have an institution or place in China, or whose income has no actual connection with the institution or place it has set up, shall be withheld at source, and the payer shall be the withholding agent. The tax shall be withheld from the payment or due payment by the withholding agent each time it is paid or due.

If the withholding agent fails to withhold the income tax that should be withheld or is unable to perform the withholding obligation according to law, the enterprise shall pay the income tax at the place where the income occurs. If an enterprise fails to pay in accordance with the law, the tax authorities may recover the tax payable of the enterprise from the amount payable by the payer of other income items within the territory of China.

Chapter

Individual Income Tax Law

Individual income tax is a kind of income tax levied mainly on all kinds of taxable income obtained by natural person. It is also a means for the government to adjust personal income with tax. The taxpayer of individual income tax includes not only individual but also the enterprise with nature of natural person. At present, China's individual income tax has initially established a combination of classification and comprehensive collection mode, namely the mixed collection system. It plays an important role in organizing fiscal revenue, improving citizens' consciousness of paying taxes, especially in adjusting the gap of individual income distribution.

5.1 Taxpayers and the Scope of Individual Income Tax

5.1.1 Taxpayers

Taxpayers include: ① Chinese citizens; ② Individual business households; ③ Sole proprietorship; ④Partnership investor; ⑤Foreign nationals (including stateless persons) and compatriots from Hong Kong Special Administrative Region, Macao Special Administrative Region and Taiwan regions who have gained employment in China.

5.1.2 Residence and Source of Income

The important factors in determining whether a person pays personal income tax in China are whether a person has a residence within China, or the length of time he has lived within China, and the source of his income.

5.1.3　Resident Taxpayer

The resident taxpayer refers to an individual who has domicile in China or does not have domicile but has resided in China for 183 days in a tax year. One tax year is the period from January 1st to December 31st of the Gregorian calendar. Resident taxpayers shall pay individual income tax in China on their taxable income, whether it is derived from sources inside or outside China.

5.1.4　Non-resident Taxpayer

Non-resident taxpayer refers to an individual who has neither domicile nor residence in China, or has no domicile and has resided in China for less than 183 days accumulatively in a tax year. Non-resident taxpayers pay individual income tax in China only on their income derived from sources in China.

5.1.5　The Tax Scope of Individual Income Tax

The tax scope of individual income tax is shown in table 5-1.

Table 5-1　The Tax Scope of Individual Income Tax

Categories of Taxable Income	Define	China Tax Residence	Non-China Tax Residence
Wages and salaries income	Wages, salaries, bonuses, end-of-year salary increases, dividends, allowances, subsidies and other income derived by individuals as a result of office or employment	Comprehensive income; It is calculated on the basis of consolidated tax year	Comprehensive income; Each item is calculated on a monthly or yearly basis
Individual service income of independent contractors	Income derived by an individual from independently performing various types of non-employment services		
Manuscript remuneration	Income derived by individuals from the publication or publication of their works in books, newspapers or periodicals		
Royalties income	Income derived by individuals from providing the right to use patent rights, trademark rights, Copyrights, non-patented technologies and other licensing rights		

Continued

Categories of Taxable Income	Define	China Tax Residence	Non-China Tax Residence
Production and business operation income earned by private-owned household enterprise	Income derived by individual industrial and commercial households from engaging in production and business operations; A sole proprietor or an individual partner of a sole proprietorship enterprise or partnership comes from the income derived from the production or operation of a sole proprietorship enterprise or partnership registered in China	Classified income; On a per capita basis	
Interest and dividends	The income from interest, dividend and bonus obtained by individuals with creditor's rights and equity		
Rental income	Income derived by individuals from the lease of real estate, machinery, equipment, vehicles and vessels and other property		
Property sales income	Income derived by individuals from the transfer of negotiable securities, stock rights, shares of property in partnership enterprises, real property, machinery, equipment, vehicles and vessels and other property		
Contingency and other income	Income derived by individuals from winning prizes, prizes, lotteries and other income of an occasional nature		

Data source: The data is summarized from the *Tax Law* (2021) textbook for the Chinese CPA Examination organized by the CICPA.

5.2　Tax Rates and Expense Deduction

China's personal income tax rates are mainly in the form of progressive tax rate and proportional tax rate. The specific tax rate and deduction standard are shown in the table 5-2.

Table 5-2　Tax Rates and Deduction Criteria

Taxable Income	Tax Rate	Permitted Standard Deduction
Wages and salaries income	Ⅶ-level progressive tax rates (3%-45%)	China Tax Residence: Annual income shall be deducted by RMB 60, 000 in expenses, special deductions, special additional deductions and other deductions determined in accordance with the law; Non-China Tax Residence: Monthly income from wages and salaries shall be deducted by RMB 5, 000 for expenses
Individual service income of independent contractors		
Manuscript remuneration		
Royalties income		

Continued

Taxable Income	Tax Rate	Permitted Standard Deduction
Production and business operation income earned by private-owned household enterprise	V-level progressive tax rates (5%-35%)	Annual gross revenue less costs, expense and loss (for the investor of partnerships and sole-proprietorships, 5, 000 yuan/month)
Interest and dividends	Rate 20%	No deduction
Rental income		Per receipt≤4, 000 yuan: fixed deduction 800 yuan Per receipt > 4, 000 yuan: deduction rate 20%
Property sales income		To deduct the original value of the property and reasonable expenses from the proceeds from the transfer of property
Contingency and other income		No deduction

Data source: The data is summarized from the *Tax Law* (2021) textbook for the Chinese CPA Examination organized by the CICPA.

5.2.1 Tax Rates Applicable to Comprehensive Income

Comprehensive income is subject to Ⅶ-level progressive tax rates, with tax rates ranging from 3% to 45% (as shown in Table 5-3).

Table 5-3   Tax Rates of Comprehensive Individual Income

Level	Annual Taxable Income Amount	Rate (%)
1	Not exceeding ￥36, 000	3
2	In excess of ￥36, 000 to ￥144, 000	10
3	In excess of ￥144, 000 to ￥300, 000	20
4	In excess of ￥300, 000 to ￥420, 000	25
5	In excess of ￥420, 000 to ￥660, 000	30
6	In excess of ￥660, 000 to ￥960, 000	35
7	In excess of ￥960, 000	45

Data source: The data is summarized from the *Tax Law* (2021) textbook for the Chinese CPA Examination organized by the CICPA.

Comprehensive income derived by individual residents in each tax year includes income from wages and salaries, remuneration for labor services, income from author's remuneration and income from royalties.

5. 2. 2   Tax Rates Applicable to Individual Service Income of Independent Contractors

Individual service income of independent contractors shall be subject to Ⅴ-level progressive tax rates for excess, with the tax rates ranging from 5% to 35% (as shown in Table 5-4).

Table 5-4　Tax Rates of Individual Service Income of Independent Contractors

Level	Annual Taxable Income Amount	Rate (%)
1	Not exceeding ¥30, 000	5
2	In excess of ¥30, 000 to ¥90, 000	10
3	In excess of ¥90, 000 to ¥300, 000	20
4	In excess of ¥300, 000 to ¥500, 000	30
5	In excess of ¥500, 000	35

Note: The annual taxable income mentioned in this table is the balance after deducting costs, expenses and losses from the total income of each tax year.

Data source: The data is summarized from the *Tax Law* (2021) textbook for the Chinese CPA Examination organized by the CICPA.

5. 2. 3   Tax Rates of Other Income

Income from interest, dividends and bonuses, income from the lease of property, income from the transfer of property and income from chance shall be taxed at a proportional rate of 20%.

5. 2. 4   Special Deduction Standard

Table 5-5　Special Deduction Standard

Item	Special Deduction Standard
Children's education	Expenses related to preschool education and academic education for children up to 3 years of age shall be deducted according to the standard quota of ¥1, 000 per month (¥12, 000 per year) for each child

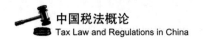

Continued

Item	Special Deduction Standard
Continuing education	During the period of academic (degree) education, ￥400 per month (￥4, 800 per year) will be deducted at a fixed rate. The taxpayer's expenses on continuing education for vocational qualifications of skilled personnel and professional and technical personnel shall be deducted according to a fixed amount of ￥3, 600 in the year when the relevant certificates are obtained
Medical treatment for serious diseases	Inside a pay taxes year, taxpayer deducts the part that medical expenses of individual burden after reimbursement of medical treatment accumulative total exceeds ￥15, 000, deduct according to the fact by taxpayer inside ￥80, 000 limit
Interest on a home loan	The first housing loan interest expense incurred by taxpayer himself or his spouse shall be deducted according to the standard quota of ￥1, 000 per month (￥12, 000 peryear). The maximum period of deduction shall not exceed 240 months (20 years). Taxpayers are only entitled to a deduction for interest on their first home loan
Housing rent	For municipalities directly under the Central Government, capital cities and cities separately listed in the plan, the deduction standard is ￥1, 500 per month (￥18, 000 per year). In addition, the registered population of more than 0.1 million in municipal districts will be deducted by ￥1, 100 per month (￥13, 200 per year); Registered population in municipal districts≤1 million, ￥800 per month (￥9, 600 per year)
Support the old	For the only child, ￥2, 000 is deducted every month (￥24, 000 per year), if the child is not an only child, the deduction shall be apportioned between the child and his/her brothers and sisters at a rate of ￥2, 000 per month (￥24, 000 per year), and the maximum amount of apportionment shall not exceed ￥1, 000 per month (￥12, 000 per year).

Data source: The data is summarized from the *Tax Law* (2021) textbook for the Chinese CPA Examination organized by the CICPA.

5.3　Tax Incentives

5.3.1　Exemptions from Individual Income Tax

(1) Awards (scholarships) in science, education, technology, culture, health, sports and environmental protection issued (promulgated) by provincial people's governments, ministries and commissions of the State Council, units above the Chinese People's Liberation Army and foreign organizations.

(2) National debt and interest on financial bonds issued by the state.

(3) Subsidies and allowances issued in accordance with the unified regulations of the state.

(4) Welfare funds, pensions and relief funds.

(5) Insurance indemnity, etc.

(6) Transfer fees and demobilization fees for servicemen.

(7) In accordance with the unified regulations of the state, the cadres and staff members shall be paid the resettlement fees, the resignation fees, the retirement wages, the retirement wages and the retirement living allowances.

(8) Income of diplomatic representatives, consular officers and other personnel of embassies and consulates of various countries in China who are exempt from tax in accordance with relevant laws of China.

(9) Income that is exempted from tax in international conventions and agreements to which the Chinese Government is a party.

(10) The housing accumulation fund, medical insurance, basic endowment insurance and unemployment insurance paid by enterprises and individuals in proportion to the rates set by the people's governments at or above the provincial level.

(11) Bonus for persons who report or assist in the investigation of various illegal or criminal acts.

(12) Individuals handling tax withholding procedures, according to the provisions of the withholding commission.

(13) Income derived by persons from the transfer of self-use premises for more than 5 years and belonging to the sole family.

5. 3. 2　Individual Foreign Income Tax is Exempt

(1) Housing subsidies, food subsidies, moving expenses and laundry expenses obtained by foreign individuals in the form of non-cash or reimbursable expenses shall be exempted from individual income tax. Foreign individuals according to reasonable standards of domestic and outside on a business trip shall be exempted from individual income tax. The fees for visiting relatives, language training and children's education obtained by foreign individuals shall be considered as reasonable parts upon examination and approval by the local

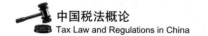

tax authorities.

(2) Income from dividends and bonuses obtained by foreign individuals from enterprises with foreign investment shall be exempted from individual income tax.

(3) Income from wages and salaries derived by foreign experts who meet any of the following conditions may be exempted from individual income tax: ①Foreign experts directly sent to work in China by the World Bank according to the *Special Loan Agreement of the World Bank*. ②Experts who were sent directly to work in our country by the United Nations' organization . ③Experts working in China for the United Nations' assistance projects. ④Experts sent to China by donor countries to work for the country's free aid projects are exempt from living allowance in addition to wages and salaries. ⑤Cultural and educational experts who have worked in China for less than 2 years according to the cultural exchange program signed by the two governments and whose wages and salaries are borne by their countries. ⑥Cultural and educational experts who have worked in China for less than 2 years under the international exchange program of Chinese colleges and universities, and whose wages and salaries are borne by the country. ⑦The salaries and salaries of experts working in China through non-governmental research agreements shall be borne by the government agencies of that country.

5.3.3   Tax Deductions for Income from Abroad

Individual residents who derive income from sources outside China may deduct from the amount of tax payable the amount of individual income tax already paid outside. However, the amount of the credit shall not exceed the tax payable of the taxpayer on his overseas income.

For income derived by individual residents within a tax year from sources outside China, the amount of income tax paid in China in accordance with the tax laws of the country (region) where the income comes from is allowed to be deducted from the amount of tax payable for that tax year within the credit limit.

The amount of tax payable on an individual resident's comprehensive income, business income and other classified income items derived from a country (region) outside China shall be the limit of his credit.

5.4　Calculation of Tax Payable

5.4.1　Calculation of Taxable Income Amount of Resident Taxpayer's Comprehensive Income

Firstly, income from wages and salaries is accounted for in full. However, income from remuneration for service and royalties shall be 80% of the income actually obtained. In addition, income from author's remuneration amounted to 56% of actual income.

Secondly, the comprehensive income of individual residents shall be the taxable income amount as the balance of the income of each tax year after deducting ￥60, 000 of expenses, special deductions, special additional deductions and other deductions determined according to law.

The formula for calculating the tax payable on individual residents' comprehensive income is as follows:

$$
\begin{aligned}
\text{Tax Payable} =\ & \text{Annual Taxable Income} \times \text{Applicable Tax Rate} - \\
& \text{Quick Calculation Deduction Number} \\
=\ & (\text{Annual Income} - ￥60,\ 000 - \text{Social Security, Housing} \\
& \text{Provident Fund Expenses} - \text{Special Additional Deduction for} \\
& \text{Enjoyment} - \text{Number of Quick Calculation Deductions}) \times \\
& \text{Applicable Tax Rate} \qquad\qquad\qquad\qquad\qquad (5-1)
\end{aligned}
$$

Table 5-6 summarizes the tax rates of residents' Comprehesive income.

Table 5-6　Tax Rates of Resident Taxpayer's Comprehensive Income

Level	Annual Taxable Income Amount	Rate (%)	Quick Calculation Deductions (yuan)
1	Not exceeding ￥36, 000	3	0
2	In excess of ￥36, 000 to ￥144, 000	10	2, 520
3	In excess of ￥144, 000 to ￥300, 000	20	16, 920
4	In excess of ￥300, 000 to ￥420, 000	25	31, 920
5	In excess of ￥420, 000 to ￥660, 000	30	52, 920

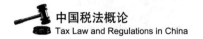

Continued

Level	Annual Taxable Income Amount	Rate （%）	Quick Calculation Deductions （yuan）
6	In excess of ￥660, 000 to ￥960, 000	35	85, 920
7	In excess of ￥960, 000	45	181, 920

Data source: The data is summarized from the *Tax Law* (2021) textbook for the Chinese CPA Examination organized by the CICPA.

• **Example 5-1**

It is assumed that an individual resident taxpayer will get a total taxable wage income of ￥120, 000 after deducting the "three insurances and one housing fund" in 2019. In addition to the special additional deduction for housing loans, the taxpayer shall not enjoy other special additional deductions or other deductions as stipulated in the tax law. Calculate the amount of personal income tax payable for the current year:

$$\text{Annual Taxable Income} = 120,000 - 60,000 - 12,000 = 48,000 \text{ yuan}$$

$$(5-2)$$

$$\text{Tax Payable} = 48,000 \times 10\% - 2,520 = 2,280 \text{ yuan} \qquad (5-3)$$

• **Example 5-2**

Assume that a certain resident individual taxpayer is the only child. After paying social security and housing provident fund in 2019, the total pretax salary income will be ￥200, 000, labor remuneration ￥10, 000, and author remuneration ￥10, 000. The taxpayer has two children and both of them are deducted from the special additional children's education. The taxpayer's parents are both living and over 60 years old. Calculate the amount of personal income tax payable for the current year:

$$\text{Annual Taxable Income} = 200,000 + 10,000 \times (1-20\%) + 10,000 \times$$
$$70\% \times (1-20\%) - 60,000 - 120,00 \times 2 - 24,000$$
$$= 213,600 - 108,000 = 105,600 \text{ yuan} \qquad (5-4)$$
$$\text{Payable Tax Amount} = 105,600 \times 10\% - 2,520 = 8,040 \text{ yuan} \qquad (5-5)$$

5.4.2 Calculation of Taxable Income Amount of Non-resident Taxpayer's Comprehensive Income

First, income from remuneration for labor services, income from author's remuneration and royalties derived by non-resident individuals is the balance of income after the deduction of 20% of expenses. The income from author's remuneration is reduced by 70%.

For income from wages and salaries of non-resident individuals, the taxable income shall be the balance of their monthly income less ¥5, 000 for expenses. For income from remuneration for labor services, income from author's remuneration and income from royalties, the amount of each income shall be the taxable income amount. The specific calculation is shown in Table 5-7.

Table 5-7　Tax Rates of Non-resident Taxpayer's Comprehensive Income

Level	Annual Taxable Income Amount	Rate （%）	Quick Calculation Deductions （yuan）
1	Not exceeding ¥3, 000	3	0
2	In excess of ¥3, 000 to ¥12, 000	10	210
3	In excess of ¥12, 000 to ¥25, 000	20	1, 410
4	In excess of ¥25, 000 to ¥35, 000	25	2, 660
5	In excess of ¥35, 000 to ¥55, 000	30	4, 410
6	In excess of ¥55, 000 to ¥80, 000	35	7, 160
7	In excess of ¥80, 000	45	15, 160

Data source: The data is summarized from the *Tax Law* （2021） textbook for the Chinese CPA Examination organized by the CICPA.

- **Example　5-3**

Assume a U. S. expert （non-resident taxpayer） working for a foreign-invested company. In February 2019, the taxable wage income of ¥10, 400 was obtained from the company. In addition, he received remuneration of ¥5, 000 from other sources. Please calculate the amount of personal income tax payable that month.

The Amount of Tax Payable on the Monthly Wage and Salary Income of the Non-
resident Individual = （10, 400-5, 000）×10%-210 = 330 yuan

$$(5-6)$$

Monthly Tax Payable on Remuneration for Labor Services of the Non-
resident Individual = 5, 000×（1-20%）×10%-210 = 190 yuan

$$(5-7)$$

5. 4. 3 Calculation of Tax Payable on Business Income

The calculation formula of the tax payable on business income is as follows:

Tax Payable = Annual Taxable Income × Applicable Tax Rate −

Quick Calculation Deduction Number or

= (Total Annual Income − Costs, Expenses and Losses) ×

Applicable Tax Rate − Quick Count Deductions　　　(5−8)

Table 5−8 shows the individual income tax rates and the number of quick calculation deductions of business income.

Table 5−8　Tax Rates of Individual Service Income of Independent Contractors

Level	Annual Taxable Income Amount	Rate (%)	Quick Calculation Deductions (yuan)
1	Not exceeding ￥30, 000	5	0
2	In excess of ￥30, 000 to ￥90, 000	10	1, 500
3	In excess of ￥90, 000 to ￥300, 000	20	10, 500
4	In excess of ￥300, 000 to ￥500, 000	30	40, 500
5	In excess of ￥500, 000	35	65, 500

Data source: The data is summarized from the *Tax Law* (2021) textbook for the Chinese CPA Examination organized by the CICPA.

The taxable income amount of production and business operations of individual industrial and commercial households shall be the balance of the total income of each tax year after deducting costs, expenses, taxes, losses and other expenditures as well as the losses of the previous year that are allowed to be made up.

Deductions and criteria:

(1) Reasonable wage and salary expenditures actually paid by individual industrial and commercial households to the employees are allowed to be deducted. The cost deduction standard for individual industrial and commercial owners shall be determined as ￥60, 000 per year. The wage and salary expenditure of individual industrial and commercial owners shall not be deducted before tax.

(2) The basic old-age insurance premium, basic medical insurance premium, unemployment insurance premium, maternity insurance premium, industrial injury insurance

premium and housing accumulation fund paid by individual industrial and commercial house-holds for their owners and employees in accordance with the provisions shall be allowed to be deducted.

(3) The trade union funds allocated and paid by individual industrial and commercial households to the local trade union organizations, the staff and workers' welfare funds actu-ally incurred and the staff and workers' education funds shall be deducted according to the facts within the standards of 2%, 14% and 2.5% of the total salary and salary respectively.

(4) Business entertainment expenses related to production and operation activities of individual industrial and commercial households shall be deducted by 60% of the actual amount, but shall not exceed 5‰ of sales (business) income in the current year at most.

Items that may not be deducted: Individual income tax; Late fees for taxation; Fines, losses of confiscated property; Donation expenditures that do not meet the deduction require-ments; Sponsorship expenses; Personal and family expenditures; Other expenses that have nothing to do with the income from production and operation are not allowed to be deducted.

5.4.4 Calculation of Tax Payable on Income from Property Lease

The income from the lease of property shall generally be the taxable income amount which shall be the balance of the income obtained by the individual each time after the fixed amount or fixed rate of deduction of the prescribed expenses. Each time income does not ex-ceed ¥4, 000, quota deducts fee ¥ 800, 20% of each income above ¥4, 000 shall be deducted at a fixed rate. The income obtained by the property lease is one time within one month.

The calculation formula of taxable income is as follows:

(1) The income does not exceed ¥ 4, 000 per time (month):

$$\text{Taxable Income} = \text{The Amount of Each (Month) Income} - \text{Allowable Deductions} -$$
$$\text{Repair Expenses (¥800 Maximum)} - ¥800 \tag{5-9}$$

(2) The income exceeds ¥4, 000 per time (month):

$$\text{Taxable Income} = [\text{The Amount of Each (Month) Income} - \text{Allowable Deductions} -$$
$$\text{Repair Expenses (¥800 Maximum)}] \times (1 - 20\%) \tag{5-10}$$

Income from the lease of property shall be subject to a proportional tax rate of 20%.

However, the individual income tax shall be temporarily reduced by 10% from January 1st, 2001 on the income derived from the individual housing rented out at the market price. The calculation formula of the tax payable is as follows:

$$\text{Tax Payable} = \text{Taxable Income} \times \text{The Applicable Tax Rate} \qquad (5\text{-}11)$$

• **Example 5-4**

Liu rented his 150-square-meter apartment to Zhang at the market price in January 2019. Liu earned a monthly rental income of ￥4,500, the annual rental income of ￥54,000. Calculate Liu's annual rental income to pay individual income tax (do not consider other taxes).

The property rental income takes the income obtained within a month as one time, and the tax rate of 10% applies to the rental of the property to the individual at the market rate. Therefore, the monthly and annual tax payable of Mr. Liu is:

$$\text{Monthly Tax Payable} = 4,500 \times (1\text{-}20\%) \times 10\% = 360 \text{ yuan} \qquad (5\text{-}12)$$
$$\text{Annual Tax Payable} = 360 \times 12 = 4,320 \text{ yuan} \qquad (5\text{-}13)$$

5.4.5 Calculation of Tax Payable on Income from Property Transfer

The formula for calculating the tax payable on the income from property transfer is:

$$\text{Tax Payable} = \text{Taxable Income} \times \text{Applicable Tax Rate} = (\text{Total Income} - $$
$$\text{Original Value of Property} - \text{Reasonable Taxes and Fees}) \times 20\%$$
$$(5\text{-}14)$$

• **Example 5-5**

A person can build a house at a cost of ￥360,000 and pay other expenses of ￥50,000. After completion, the man sold the house for ￥600,000. In the process of selling the house in accordance with the provisions to pay transaction fees and other related taxes and fees ￥35,000. The calculation process of the individual income tax payable is as follows:

$$\text{Taxable Income} = \text{Income from Property Transfer} - \text{Original Value of Property} - $$
$$\text{Reasonable Expenses} = 600,000 - (360,000 + 50,000) - 35,000 = 155,000 \text{ yuan}$$
$$(5\text{-}15)$$

$$\text{Tax Payable} = 155,000 \times 20\% = 31,000 \text{ yuan} \tag{5-16}$$

5.4.6 Calculation of Tax Payable on Interest, Dividend, Bonus Income and Contingent Income

The formula for calculating the tax payable on interest, dividend, bonus income and contingent income is as follows:

$$\text{Tax Payable} = \text{Taxable Income} \times \text{Applicable Tax Rate} = \text{The Amount of Each Income} \times 20\% \tag{5-17}$$

5.4.7 Final Settlement

After the end of each year, individual residents shall summarize the amount of their four comprehensive incomes, including wages and salaries, remuneration for labor services, author's remuneration and royalties, which they received on January 1st, solstice and December 31st of the current year. After deducting ￥60,000 of expenses, special deductions, special additional deductions, other deductions determined according to law and eligible public welfare and charity donations, the comprehensive individual income tax rate shall apply and the number of quick calculation deductions shall be deducted. And calculate the final amount of tax payable in this year, and then deduct the amount of tax paid in advance in this year, and get the amount of tax refunded or payable in this year. Finally declare to tax authority and deal with drawback or compensatory duty. The specific calculation formula is as follows:

$$\begin{aligned}
\text{Annual Tax Refundable or Supplementary Payable} = [\ & (\text{The Amount of} \\
& \text{Comprehensive Income} - ￥60,000 - \text{Special Deductions for} \\
& \text{``Three Insurances and One Housing Fund''} - \text{Special Additional} \\
& \text{Deductions for Children's Education} - \text{Other Deductions Determined} \\
& \text{According to Law} - \text{donations}) \times \text{Applicable Tax Rate} - \text{Number of} \\
& \text{Quick-count deductions}] - \text{The Amount of Tax Paid in Advance This Year}
\end{aligned} \tag{5-18}$$

5. 5   Individual Income Tax Declaration

The individual income tax payment method, implements the two methods of self-declaration for the taxpayers and the withholding and declaration for all taxpayers.

5. 5. 1   Self-reporting by Individual Taxpayers

Self-declaration and tax payment is to declare the taxable income items and amount to the tax authorities within the tax payment period stipulated by the tax law by the taxpayer, fill in the individual income tax return truthfully, and calculate the payable tax amount according to the tax law provisions, which is a method of paying personal income tax accordingly.

Taxpayers shall file tax returns in accordance with law under any of the following circumstances:

(1) The acquisition of comprehensive income need to be settled.

(2) There is no withholding agent for taxable income.

(3) When taxable income is obtained and the withholding agent fails to withhold the tax.

(4) Obtaining income from abroad.

(5) The cancellation of Chinese household registration due to emigration.

(6) Non-resident individuals within the territory of China obtain the income from wages and salaries from two or more places.

(7) Other circumstances stipulated by the State Council.

Table 5-9 shows the declaration of individual income tax.

Table 5-9   Declaration of Individual Income Tax

Tax Returns	Advance Payment of Tax and Declaration	Final Settlement or Summary Declaration	Declaration Place
Residents' personal comprehensive income	The income shall be withheld and prepaid within 15 days of the next month	Income was earned the following March 1st by solstice on June 30th	The location of the employer

Continued

Tax Returns	Advance Payment of Tax and Declaration	Final Settlement or Summary Declaration	Declaration Place
Operating income	Advance payment by month: The advance payment tax declaration shall be made within 15 days after the end of each month. Quarterly advance payment: Tax advance declaration shall be made within 15 days after the end of each quarter	Before March 31st of the next year	Location of operation and management
Foreign income	—	Income was earned the following March 1st by solstice on June 30th	The location of the employer
Chinese household registration shall be cancelled for emigration		Before applying for cancellation of Chinese household registration	Domicile place
A non-China tax resident individual obtains two or more salaries within the territory of China	Declaration of income within 15 days of the next month		One of the places where the office or employer is located

Data source: The data is summarized from the *Tax Law* (2021) textbook for the Chinese CPA Examination organized by the CICPA.

5.5.2 Settlement of Consolidated Income

A taxpayer who has obtained comprehensive income and meets one of the following circumstances shall complete the final settlement according to law:

(1) Obtain comprehensive income from two or more sources, and the balance of comprehensive income after deducting special deductions exceeds ￥60, 000.

(2) Obtain one or more of income from remuneration , labor remuneration, and royalties, and the balance of the comprehensive annual income minus special deductions exceeds ￥60, 000.

(3) Below payable tax within the tax year.

(4) Taxpayers apply for tax refund.

5.5.3　Tax Returns for Business Income Obtained

Income from business operations derived by owners of individual businesses, investors in sole proprietorships, individual partners in partnerships, individual leaseholders and other individuals engaged in production or business operations includes the following circumstances:

(1) Income derived from production and business activities of individual industrial and commercial households, as well as the income derived from production and business operations of sole proprietorship enterprises and individual partners of partnership enterprises registered in China.

(2) Income derived by individuals from their engagement in running schools, medical treatment, consultation and other paid service in accordance with the law.

(3) Income derived by individuals from contracted or leased operation of enterprises or institutions, as well as the income from subcontracting or subleasing.

(4) Income derived by individuals from their engagement in other production and business activities.

5.5.4　Tax Returns for Non-Resident Individuals

Non-resident individuals who have obtained income from wages and salaries, remuneration for labor services, author's remuneration or royalties shall, before June 30st of the following year, file tax returns with the local competent tax authorities where the withholding agent is located. And submit the individual income tax return (Form A).

If two or more withholding agents fail to withhold tax, they shall choose to file tax returns with the local competent tax authorities where the withholding agent is located.

If a non-resident individual leaves China before June 30st of the following year (except for temporary departure from China), he/she shall file a tax return before leaving China.

Chapter

6

Resource Tax Law and Environmental Protection Tax Law

6. 1　Resource Tax Law

6. 1. 1　Definition

Resource tax is a general term of the taxes on natural resources. The level-difference resource tax is a tax of the country's contribution to the development and utilization of natural resources. The general resource tax is a state-to-state resource, such as urban land, mineral, water flow, forest, mountain ridge, grassland, waste land, tidal flat, etc. as stipulated in the constitution of our country, and it is a tax that is levied in order to obtain the right to use the taxable resources.

According to *Provisional Regulations of the People's Republic of China on Resource Tax*, taxable resources cover two broad categories: mineral products and salt. The first category includes crude oil, natural gas, coal, other non-metal ores, ferrous metal ores and non-ferrous metal ores while the second includes solid salt and liquid salt.

Natural resources are rich in varieties. China, however, presently only levies the resource tax on those businesses engaged in the exploitation of taxable mineral products and the production of salt. Tax is computed on the basis of the quantities of taxable resources sold or self-consumed.

The resource tax is mainly levied for adjusting differential income derived from resources. The resource tax with reasonably discriminate rates is imposed to collect that revenue of different grades so that competition on a relatively equal footing is promoted for those resource exploitation and utilization businesses.

There are differences in tax payment in different regions in China.

6. 1. 2　Characteristics

(1) In our country, the scope of resource tax is narrow, only the difference of partial differential income is large, the resources are more common, and the mineral products and

salt which are easy to collect and manage are listed as the scope of taxation. With the rapid development of China's economy, the rational utilization and effective protection of natural resources will become more and more important. Therefore, the tax scope of resource tax should be gradually expanded. The scope of China's resource tax includes mineral products and salt.

(2) The differential tax rate was levied on July 1st, 2016, and China implemented the reform of resource tax, and the method of resource tax collection was changed.

(3) The implementation of source collection, whether or not the mining or production units belong to independent accounting, the resource tax is stipulated in the source control of the mining or production area, which not only takes into account the interests of the excavated land, but also avoids the loss of tax. This is different from the uniform payment of other taxes by independent units.

6.1.3 Role

Adjusting the differential income of resources is beneficial to the competition of enterprises at the same level. Strengthening the management of resources is helpful to promote the rational development of enterprises and make use of. In conjunction with other taxes, it is conducive to giving full play to the overall function of tax leverage. It is a tax levied on the exploitation and utilization of national mineral resources. The purpose of levying resource tax is to make the differential income with superior natural resources conditions owned by the state and to eliminate the unreasonable distribution of profits caused by the advantages and disadvantages of resources.

6.1.4 Tax Regulations

(1) The resource tax taxpayer refers to the units and individuals that exploit taxable mineral products or produce salt in China.

(2) Resource tax withholding agent. In some cases, taxes may be withheld on behalf of the units that acquire non-taxable mineral products.

(3) Scope of resource tax collection is crude oil, natural gas, coal, other non-metallic ores, black metal ores, nonferrous metal ores and salts.

6.1.5　Collection Management

Resource tax shall be declared and paid monthly or quarterly. If the payment cannot be made within a fixed period of time, the payment may be made according to the time of filing.

Resource tax is calculated and paid in the sales or self-use of taxable products. If a taxpayer directly processes a non-taxable product from a self-mined raw ore or continuously produces a non-taxable product from a concentrate processed by the self-mined raw ore, the resource tax shall be calculated and paid in the link of transferring the raw ore or the concentrated ore.

Taxpayers shall report and pay resource tax to the tax authorities of the place where the taxable products are mined or produced.

6.2　Environmental Protection Tax Law

6.2.1　Definition

The Environmental Protection Tax Law of the People's Republic of China was adopted by the 25th Meeting of the Standing Committee of the 12th National People's Congress of the People's Republic of China on December 25th, 2016. After the strictest environmental inspection, *the Environmental Protection Tax Law of the People's Republic of China* was put into force on January 1st, 2018.

The government started to levy environmental protection taxes. This turns those public institutions and other production managers to environmental tax payers. According to the law, for the enterprises, public institutions and other producers and operators that directly discharge taxable air, water pollutants and solid wastes as well as noise pollution shall pay environmental pollution tax. And this includes most of the manufacturing industries and processing industries that cause severe pollution.

This law is formulated in order to protect and improve the environment, reduce pollutant emissions and promote the construction of ecological civilization. In the territory of China and other sea areas under the jurisdiction of China, enterprises and institutions that directly discharge taxable pollutants to the environment and other producers and operators shall pay environmental protection taxes in accordance with the provisions of this law. The term "taxable pollutants" as mentioned in this law refers to air pollutants, water pollutants, solid waste and noise specified in the tax schedule for environmental protection tax items.

Under any of the following circumstances, it shall not discharge pollutants directly into the environment and shall not pay the environmental protection tax for the corresponding pollutants:

(1) Enterprises, institutions and other producers and operators shall centrally treat sewage established in accordance with the law and discharge taxable pollutants from places where domestic waste is centrally treated.

(2) Enterprises, institutions and other producers and operators store or dispose of solid waste at facilities and places shall meet the national and local environmental protection standards.

6.2.2　Role

Environmental protection tax is a good protection for international trade. Those public institutions and other production managers that directly discharge taxable pollutants are taxpayers instead of pollution charges which have been put into force for nearly 40 years. This fee-to-tax policy will influence 5 million enterprises.

Unlike pollutant charges, the government has added extra conditions for tax reduction. Taxpayers shall pay 75% of the gross if the effluent air pollutants or water pollutants are 30% lower than the required standard. Meanwhile, the emission reduction reward is reserved. If the taxpayers discharge air pollutants or water pollutants with the gross 50% lower than the required standard, the taxes will be halved.

Scope: Air pollutants, water pollutants, solid waste and noise pollutants.

Specific industries include: thermal power, steelworks, coal, metallurgy, construction materials, textile manufacturing, textile printing, paper making, food processing, chemical engineering, pharmacy, such pollution industries as well as leading raw materials factory, chemical plants and other supporting enterprises like painting factories, tire factories, plastic plants and so on.

6.2.3   Basis and Amount of Tax Payable

(1) The tax basis of the taxable pollutant shall be determined in accordance with the following methods: ①The amount of pollution equivalent to the pollutant emission is determined by the taxable atmospheric pollutants; ②The amount of the taxable water pollutant is determined according to the amount of pollution equivalent to the pollutant discharge amount; ③The taxable solid waste shall be determined in accordance with the discharge of solid waste; ④The taxable noise shall be determined in decibels above the national standard. Taxable atmospheric pollutants, the number of pollution equivalent of the water pollutants, the amount of the pollutant's discharge divided by the pollution of the pollutant shall be calculated as the magnitude.

(2) Water pollutants and solid wastes shall be calculated in accordance with the following methods and sequences: ①The taxpayer is installed and used the automatic monitoring equipment for pollutants in accordance with the national regulations and monitoring specifications, and shall be calculated according to the automatic monitoring data of the pollutants; ②Where the taxpayer does not install the automatic monitoring equipment for pollutants, the monitoring data shall be calculated in accordance with the relevant national regulations and monitoring specifications issued by the monitoring institution; ③If there is no monitoring condition due to the number of discharged pollutants and other reasons, it should be calculated according to the sewage discharge coefficient and the material balance calculation method specified by the ecological environment competent department of the State Council; ④ It cannot be calculated in accordance with the methods specified in Items 1 to 3 of this Article, in accordance with the provinces and autonomous regions.

(3) The amount of tax payable for environmental protection shall be calculated as follows: ①The amount of the taxable atmospheric pollutant shall be the amount of pollution equivalent multiplied by the specific applicable tax amount; ②The amount of the taxable water pollutant shall be the amount of pollution equivalent multiplied by the specific applicable tax amount; ③The amount of the taxable solid waste shall be the amount of solid waste multiplied by the specific applicable tax amount; ④The amount of taxable noise shall be in

excess of the specific applicable tax amount corresponding to the decibel number of the national standard.

6.2.4   Tax Standard

The rates of environmental protection tax in China is shown in table 6−1.

Table 6−1   The Rates of Environmental Protection Tax in China

Taxable Items		Tax Unit	Tax Amounts
Air pollutants		Per pollutant equivalent	¥1.2−¥12
Water pollutants		Per Pollutional equivalent	¥1.4−¥14
Solid waste	Coal gangue	Per ton	¥5
	Tailings	Per ton	¥15
	Hazardous waste	Per ton	¥1,000
	Smelting slag, flyash, slag, other solid waste	Per ton	¥25
Noise	Industrial noise	Exceed 1−3 decibel	¥350 per month
		Exceed 4−6 decibel	¥700 per month
		Exceed 7−9 decibel	¥1,400 per month
		Exceed 10−12 decibel	¥2,800 per month
		Exceed 13−15 decibel	¥5,600 per month
		Exceed 16 decibel	¥11,200 per month

Data source: The data is summarized from the *Tax Law* (2021) textbook for the Chinese CPA Examination organized by the CICPA.

6.2.5   Collection Management

Taxpayers shall faithfully file tax returns in accordance with the law and bear responsibility for the authenticity and completeness of the tax returns. Tax authorities collect and administer environmental taxes. The competent departments of environmental protection administration shall monitor and administer pollutants.

The competent department of environmental protection administration shall regularly submit to the tax authority information related to environmental protection such as the pollutant discharge permits, pollutant discharge data of the pollutant discharging units, environmental violations and administrative penalties.

Tax authorities shall regularly submit to the competent department of environmental protection tax information concerning environmental protection tax, such as tax returns of taxpayers, tax storage, tax reduction and exemption, tax arrears and risk doubts.

Tax authorities shall compare the tax return data and data of taxpayers with the relevant data and data submitted by the competent department of environmental protection administration.

Where a tax authority finds that the data and data of a taxpayer's tax return are abnormal or that the taxpayer fails to file a tax return within the prescribed time limit, it may refer the matter to the competent department of environmental protection administration for review.

The tax obligation of environmental protection tax occurs on the day when the taxpayer discharges taxable pollutants. Environmental protection tax is calculated monthly and declared quarterly. If the payment cannot be made within a fixed period of time, the payment may be made according to the time of filing.

Taxpayers shall report and pay environmental protection tax to the tax authorities of the place where the taxable pollutants are discharged. The place where the taxable pollutants are discharged refers to the place where the taxable air pollutants, water pollutants discharge outlets, taxable solid wastes and taxable noise are produced.

Chapter

7

Laws of Property Taxes

7.1 Real Estate Tax Law

Real estate tax is a kind of tax levied on the owner or operator of real estate according to the price or rental income of real estate.

7.1.1 The Scope and Tax Object of Real Estate Tax

7.1.1.1 The Scope of Real Estate Tax

The scopes are including cities, counties, towns and industrial and mining areas. Houses located in rural areas are not taxed for the time being.

7.1.1.2 The Tax Object of Real Estate Tax is Real Estate

The so-called real estate refers to a place with a roof and enclosure structure (with walls or columns on both sides), which can shelter from the wind and rain, and can be used for people to produce, study, work, entertain, live or store materials.

7.1.2 Taxpayers

The taxpayer of real estate tax is the property owner of the house. In which: ①Property rights belong to the state, and its management units and individuals are taxpayers; ②If the property right is pawned, the mortgagee is the taxpayer; ③If the property owner or mortgagee is not in the place where the property is located, or if the property right is undetermined and the rent dispute is unresolved, the property custodian or user is a taxpayer.

7.1.3 Tax Basis

The taxable basis of real estate tax is the taxable value of the property or the rental income of the property. According to the taxable value of the property, it is called ad valorem levy. According to the real estate rental income levy, it is called from the rent levy.

7.1.3.1 Ad Valorem Levy

It refers to the residual value of the property as the tax basis. The residual value of real estate is the residual value after deducting 10% – 30% from the original value of real estate. The specific deduction range shall be decided by the people's governments of provinces, autonomous regions and municipalities directly under the Central Government. The determination of deduction range should take into account both the natural loss of houses and the value-added factors of houses.

7.1.3.2 From the Rent Levied

It refers to the rental income from housing rental as the tax basis. Rental income is the remuneration obtained by the owner of the property right to rent out the right to use the property, including monetary income and income in kind. If the rent income is offset by labor or other forms of remuneration, a standard rent amount shall be determined according to the rent level of similar local real estate.

7.1.4 Tax Rates

Production tax adopts proportional tax rate. There are two tax rates:

(1) If the residual value of the original value of the property is deducted by 10% – 30%, the tax rate is 1.2%.

(2) According to the rental income of housing rental, the tax rate is 12%. (The real estate tax is levied at the rate of 4% for individual rental housing, regardless of use. For enterprises, public institutions, social organizations and other organizations renting houses for living to individuals at market prices, the real estate tax will be levied at a reduced rate of 4%.)

7.1.5 Tax Incentive

Real estate tax relief projects mainly include: ①Property occupied by state organs, people's organizations and the army; ②The real estate occupied by the unit that allocates the business funds by the financial department; ③Religious temples, parks, places of interest for their own use of real estate; ④Non-business properties owned by individuals;

Chapter 7   Laws of Property Taxes

⑤Other properties approved by the Ministry of Finance for tax exemption.

7.2   Deed Tax Law

Deed tax refers to a kind of tax levied on units and individuals who have obtained land use rights and housing ownership in the process of transferring the ownership of land use rights and housing ownership. Its characteristic is that taxpayers are property rights bearers. It adopts proportional tax rate and belongs to local tax. The significance of levying deed tax increases local fiscal revenue and accumulates funds for local economic construction. It helps regulate the real estate market, standardize market transactions, protect the legitimate rights and interests of property owners, and reduce property disputes.

7.2.1   The Tax Object of Deed Tax

It is the land where the right to use is transferred and the house where the ownership is transferred.

7.2.1.1   The Specific Content of the Tax Object

(1) Transfer of state-owned land use rights.

(2) Transfer of land use rights.

(3) sale, gift and exchange of houses.

7.2.1.2   As the Transfer of Land Use Rights, Housing Sales or Housing Donation Behavior

(1) Invest and buy shares at the price of land and housing ownership, and pay off debts with land and housing ownership.

(2) Inheriting the ownership of land and houses in the form of intangible assets.

(3) Accept the ownership of land and houses by winning awards.

(4) To inherit the ownership of land and houses by means of pre-purchase or prepaid fund-raising for building houses.

(5) Other ways of transferring land and housing ownership determined by the Ministry

of Finance according to the *Provisional Regulations of the People's Republic of China on Deed Tax*.

7.2.2 Taxpayers

Taxpayers of deed tax refer to the units and individuals who bear the ownership of land and houses transferred in China. Domestic territory refers to the administrative jurisdiction within which the People's Republic of China implements actual taxation. Land and housing ownership refers to land use rights and housing ownership. Units refer to enterprises, institutions, state organs, military units, social organizations and other organizations. Individuals refer to self-employed persons and other individuals, including Chinese citizens and foreigners.

7.2.3 The Tax Basis of Deed Tax

It's the price of real estate. There are the following situations:

(1) The transfer of the state-owned land use right, the sale of the land use right, and housing sales are with the transaction price as the tax basis.

(2) The tax basis of the grant of land use right and the grant of house shall be verified by the tax collection authority with reference to the market price of the sale of local land use right and house.

(3) The tax basis for land use rights exchange and housing exchange is the price difference between the exchanged land use rights and housing, that is, when the exchange prices are equal, the deed tax shall be exempted. If the exchange price is not equal, the overpaid party shall pay the deed tax.

(4) The tax basis for obtaining the land use right by means of allocation and approving the transfer of real estate shall be paid by the real estate transferor for the charge for land use right or land income.

7.2.4 Tax Rates

It implements a proportional tax rate of 3%-5%. The specific applicable tax rate shall be determined by the people's governments of provinces, autonomous regions and munici-palities directly under the Central Government within the scope according to the actual situa-tion of each place. For individuals who purchase ordinary housing, and the housing belongs to the only housing of the family (the members include the purchaser, spouse and minor children), the deed tax will be levied by half. If an individual purchases ordinary housing of 90 square meters or less, and the housing belongs to the only family housing, the deed tax will be levied at a reduced rate of 1%.

7.2.5　Tax Incentive

The reduction and exemption policy of deed tax mainly includes the following aspects:

(1) State organs, institutions, social organizations and military units that bear land and houses for office, education, medical care, scientific research and military facilities shall be exempted from deed tax.

(2) Urban workers shall purchase public housing for the first time according to regula-tions, and shall be exempted from deed tax.

(3) If the house is re-purchased due to the loss of the house for force majeure, it shall be reduced as appropriate.

(4) If the land and houses are expropriated and occupied by the people's governments at or above the county level and the ownership of the land and houses is re-accepted, the provincial people's government shall determine whether to reduce or exempt them.

(5) Those who bear the land use rights of barren hills, gullies and wasteland and are used for agriculture, forestry, animal husbandry and fishery production shall be exempted from deed tax.

(6) As confirmed by the Ministry of Foreign Affairs of the People's Republic of China, foreign embassies, consulates, agencies of United Nations in China and their diplomatic rep-resentatives, consular officials and other diplomats who should be exempted from taxes shall bear the ownership of land and houses in accordance with the relevant laws and regulations of China and bilateral treaties or agreements concluded or acceded to by China, and shall be exempted from deed tax.

Taxpayers whose tax reduction or exemption have been approved above shall pay the tax exempted or reduced in full if they change the use of the land and houses, and no longer fall

within the scope of tax reduction or exemption.

7.3　Urban Land Use Tax Law

Urban land use tax is a kind of tax calculated and levied according to the prescribed tax amount for units and individuals occupying urban land, taking the actual occupied land area as the tax basis. It is of great significance to levy urban land use tax, which can promote the rational allocation and economical use of land resources and improve land use efficiency. It is conducive to adjusting land differential income, creating a fair competitive environment for land users, and promoting enterprises to strengthen economic accounting. It is beneficial to straighten out the distribution relationship between the state and land users.

7.3.1　The Tax Scope and Taxpayer

(1) The scopes of taxation include cities, counties, towns and industrial and mining areas.

(2) The taxpayer refers to the units and individuals who use land within cities, counties, towns and industrial and mining areas. Specifically, it includes: ①Units and individuals with land use rights; ②Units and individuals with land use rights are not located in the land, and the actual users and custodians of the land are taxpayers; ③If the land use right is not determined or the ownership dispute is not resolved, the actual user is the taxpayer; ④If the land use right is shared, all parties are taxpayers, and all parties pay taxes separately.

7.3.2　The Tax Basis

Tax basis is the land area actually occupied by taxpayers.

The land area actually occupied by taxpayers is determined according to the following methods:

(1) Where the units determined by the people's governments of provinces, autono-

mous regions and municipalities directly under the Central Government organize the measurement of land area, the measured area shall prevail.

(2) The survey has not been organized, but the taxpayer holds the land use certificate issued by the government department, and the land area confirmed by the certificate shall prevail.

(3) If the land use certificate has not been issued, the taxpayer shall declare the land area and pay taxes accordingly. Adjustments will be made after the land use certificate is issued.

7.3.3　Tax Rates

Urban land use tax adopts the fixed tax rate of regional difference, and the annual tax payable of land use tax per square meter is stipulated respectively according to large, medium and small cities, county towns, administrative towns and industrial and mining areas.

The annual amount of land use tax per square meter is as follows: ①1.5 yuan to 30 yuan in big cities; ②1.2 yuan to 24 yuan in medium-sized cities; ③0.9 yuan to 18 yuan in small cities; ④0.6 yuan to 12 yuan in counties, towns, and industrial and mining areas.

7.4　Travel Tax Law

Travel tax is levied on the owners or managers of vehicles and ships in the People's Republic of China. The significance of collection is to open up local financial resources and raise funds for local finance, regulate the distribution of wealth and promote social equity, strengthen the use and management of vehicles and vessels.

7.4.1　Taxpayers

The taxpayer of travel tax is the owner or manager of the vehicles and vessels (hereinafter referred to as "vehicles and vessels") within the territory of the People's Republic of China.

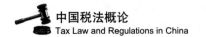

7.4.2   The Tax Base and Tax Rates

The tax base is classified into two categories respectively for vehicles and vessels, and one defining characteristic of travel tax is that it is a quantity tax: The tax base for vehicles is the number of the taxable vehicles or the net-tonnage of the taxable vehicles; The tax base for vessels is the net-tonnage or the length of the taxable vessels. The travel tax shall be filed and paid on a yearly basis. The annual amount of tax payable is separately computed for vehicles and vessels.

There are five major tax items, passenger vehicles, commercial vehicles, other vehicles, motorcycles and vessels. The annual tax amount standards of the tax items vary from RMB 36-5, 400/vehicle, or from RMB 3-60/ton in terms of dead weight (net tonnage), or from RMB 600-2, 000/m in terms of the length of yacht body. You can refer to the table 7-1 for more detail.

Table 7-1   Tax Rates of Travel Tax

	Tax Items	Units	Tax Amount (yuan)	Remarks
Passenger cars are classified by engine cylinder capacity (displacement volume)	1. 0 liter (inclusive) or less	Per car	60-360	The number of passengers is less than 9 (inclusive)
	1. 0-1. 6 liters (inclusive)		300-540	
	1. 6-2. 0 liters (inclusive)		360-660	
	2. 0-2. 5 liters (inclusive)		660-1, 200	
	2. 5-3. 0 liters (inclusive)		1, 200-2, 400	
	3. 0-4. 0 liters (inclusive)		2, 400-3, 600	
	4. 0 liters or more		3, 600-5, 400	
Commercial vehicle	bus	Per unit	480-1, 440	1. Including semi-trailer tractors, trailers, passenger and cargo vehicles, three-wheeled vehicles and low-speed cargo vehicles.
	truck	Curb weight Per ton	16-120	2. The tax of trailer is calculated at 50% of the truck

Continued

	Tax Items	Units	Tax Amount (yuan)	Remarks
Other vehicles	Special motor vehicle	Curb weight Per ton	16-120	Excluding tractor
	Wheeled mobiel machinery for special purpose	Curb weight Per ton	16-120	
Motorcycle		Per unit	36-180	
Vessel	Power-driven vessel	Net tonnage Per ton	3-6	The tax of tugs and non-motorized barges shall be calculated at 50% of the motorized vessel
	Yacht	Length Per meter	600-2, 000	

Data source: The data is summarized from the *Tax Law* (2021) textbook for the Chinese CPA Examination organized by the CICPA.

It is interesting to note that in the table a range for each type of vehicles and vessels is specified instead of a number.

7.4.3　Calculation of Tax Payable

For the new vehicles and vessels, the tax payable in the year shall be calculated on a monthly basis from the month in which the tax liability occurs.

The calculation formula is:

$$\text{Tax Payable} = (\text{Annual Tax Payable} \div 12) \times \text{Number of Taxable Months}$$

$$(7\text{-}1)$$

$$\text{The Number of Taxable Months} = 12 - \text{The Time When the Tax Liability Occurs}$$
$$(\text{Take the Month}) + 1$$

$$(7\text{-}2)$$

7.4.4　Tax Incentive

The following vehicles and vessels are exempt from travel tax: ①Fishing boats for fishing or breeding; ②Vehicles and vessels specially used by the army and armed police forces; ③Police vehicles and vessels; ④The national comprehensive fire control and rescue vehicles and the national comprehensive fire control and rescue ships with the special license plates for emergency rescue; ⑤Vehicles and vessels of foreign embassies and consulates in China, representative offices of international organizations in China and their relevant personnel that should be exempted from tax in accordance with the law; ⑥Travel tax may be reduced or exempted for vehicles and vessels that save energy and use new energy. If it is difficult to pay taxes due to serious natural disasters and there are other special reasons that really need to be reduced or exempted, the travel tax may be reduced or exempted.

7.4.5 The Administration of Travel Tax

(1) The tax payment place of travel tax is the registration place of travel or the place where the travel tax withholding agent is located. For vehicles and vessels that do not need to be registered in accordance with the law, the tax payment place of travel tax is the place where the owner or manager of the vehicle and vessel tax is located.

(2) The time when the travel tax obligation occurs is the month in which the ownership or management right of the travel is obtained.

(3) Travel tax is reported and paid annually. The specific tax reporting period shall be stipulated by the people's governments of provinces, autonomous regions and municipalities directly under the Central Government.

(4) Public security, transportation, agriculture, fisheries and other travel registration management departments, ship inspection agencies and travel tax withholding agent industry authorities should be in the provision of travel related information, to assist the tax authorities to strengthen the management of travel tax collection.

(5) The owner or manager of the vehicle shall submit a certificate of tax payment or exemption in accordance with the law to the traffic administrative department of the public security organ when applying for the registration and regular inspection of the vehicle. The traffic control department of the public security organ shall go through the relevant formalities after verification.

Chapter

8

Laws of Behavior Taxes

8.1　Land Appreciation Tax Law

8.1.1　Taxpayers and Scope of Taxation

8.1.1.1　Taxpayer

All units and individuals who purchase automobiles, trams, vehicle trailers and motorcycles within the territory of China shall be liable to pay vehicle purchase tax.

8.1.1.2　Scope of Taxation

The vehicle purchase tax takes the listed vehicles as the tax object, and the vehicles not listed are not taxed. The specific provisions are as follows: ①Cars, including all kinds of cars; ②Motorcycle; ③Tram; ④Trailer; ⑤Farm Transporter.

8.1.2　Tax Rate and Tax Base

8.1.2.1　Tax Rate

The vehicle purchase tax adopts a unified proportional tax rate, and the tax rate is 10%.

8.1.2.2　Tax Base

The taxable price of the taxable vehicle purchased by the taxpayer shall be the total price actually paid by the taxpayer to the seller, excluding the value-added tax. The taxable price of taxable vehicles imported by taxpayers for their own use shall be the customs value plus customs duties and consumption tax. The taxable price of a taxpayer's self-produced and self-used taxable vehicle shall be determined according to the sales price of the same type of taxable vehicle produced by the taxpayer, excluding value-added tax. The taxable price of the taxable vehicle for its own use obtained by the taxpayer by gift, award or other means shall be determined according to the price stated in the relevant certificate when purchasing the taxable vehicle, excluding the value-added tax.

8. 1. 3　Calculation of Tax Payable

The vehicle purchase tax adopts the method of ad valorem fixed rate to calculate the tax payable：

$$\text{Tax Payable} = \text{Tax Base} \times \text{Tax Rate} \tag{8-1}$$

8. 1. 3. 1　Calculation of Tax Payable on Purchase of Self-use Taxable Vehicles

• **Example　8-1**

In May 2020, Mr. Song purchased a car for his own use from an Automobile Co. , Ltd. , and paid 226, 000 yuan including VAT, 580 yuan for collecting temporary license fee, 1, 000 yuan for collecting insurance fee, 4, 000 yuan for purchasing tools and spare parts, and 1, 200 yuan for vehicle decoration. The payment is made by the Automobile Co. , Ltd. to issue a "unified invoice for motor vehicle sales" and related bills. Please calculate the vehicle purchase tax payable by Mr. Song.

$$\text{Tax Base} = (226, 000 + 580 + 1, 000 + 4, 000 + 1, 200)/(1 + 13\%)$$
$$= 206, 000 \text{ yuan} \tag{8-2}$$

$$\text{Tax Payable} = 206, 000 \times 10\% = 20, 600 \text{ yuan} \tag{8-3}$$

8. 1. 3. 2　Calculation of Tax Payable on Imported Self-use Taxable Vehicles

The formula for calculating the tax payable of taxable vehicles imported by taxpayers for their own use is as follows：

$$\text{Tax Payable} = (\text{Customs Value} + \text{Tariff} + \text{Consumption Tax}) \times \text{Tax Rate} \tag{8-4}$$

• **Example　8-2**

In August 2018, a foreign trade import and export company imported 10 cars of a certain model from abroad. When the company declared to import these cars, the Customs at the place of declaration examined the relevant declaration materials and determined that the customs value was 185, 000 yuan per car. According to the customs policy, the customs collected 46, 200 yuan per car, and collected 25, 600 yuan of consumption tax and 41, 000 yuan of value-added tax for each car according to the relevant provisions of consumption tax and value-added tax. According to the above data, calculate the vehicle purchase tax payable.

$$\text{Tax Base} = 185,000 + 46,200 + 25,600 = 256,800 \text{ yuan} \qquad (8\text{-}5)$$
$$\text{Tax Payable} = 256,800 \times 10\% = 25,680 \text{ yuan} \qquad (8\text{-}6)$$

8.1.4 Tax Incentive

The vehicles used by foreign embassies, consulates, international organizations and their diplomatic personnel in China are tax-free.

8.2 Farmland Occupation Tax Law

8.2.1 Taxpayer and Tax Scope

8.2.1.1 Taxpayer

The taxpayer of farmland occupation tax refers to the units and individuals who occupy cultivated land to construct buildings and structures or engage in non-agricultural construction within the territory of the People's Republic of China.

8.2.1.2 Scope of Taxation

The tax scope of farmland occupation tax includes the cultivated land occupied by taxpayers for housing or other cultivated land owned by the state and collective for non-agricultural construction.

The term "farmland" mentioned in the farmland occupation tax refers to the land used for planting crops, including garden, woodland, grassland, farmland and water conser-

vancy land, aquaculture water surface, etc.

8.2.2 Tax Rates and Tax Base

8.2.2.1 Tax Rates

In the tax rate design of farmland occupation tax, the regional differential fixed tax rate is adopted. The tax rates are as follows:

(1) In the area where the per capita cultivated land is less than 1 mu, it is 10-50 yuan per square meter.

(2) In the area of cultivated land per capita more than 2 mu but not more than 3 mu, it is 8-40 yuan per square meter.

(3) In the area of cultivated land per capita more than 1 mu but not more than 2 mu, it is 8-40 yuan per square meter.

(4) In the area of cultivated land per capita more than 3 mu per capita, it is 5-25 yuan per square meter.

If basic farmland is occupied, an additional 150% of the applicable tax shall be levied.

8.2.2.2 Tax Base

The farmland occupation tax is calculated on the basis of the area of the land actually occupied by the taxpayer which belongs to the tax scope of the farmland occupation tax (hereinafter referred to as "the taxable land"), and the tax shall be calculated according to the local applicable tax amount of the taxable land, and shall be collected in one time.

8.2.3 Calculation of Tax Payable

The taxable amount of farmland occupation tax is the area of taxable land occupied by the taxpayer (square meters) multiplied by the applicable tax amount. The calculation formula is as follows:

$$\text{Tax Payable} = \text{Taxable Land Area} \times \text{Applicable Tax} \qquad (8-7)$$

• **Example   8-3**

Suppose that an enterprise in a city newly occupies 20, 000 square meters of cultivated land for industrial construction, and the quota tax rate applicable to the cultivated land occupied is 20 yuan/square meter. Calculate the farmland occupation tax payable by the enterprise.

$$\text{Tax Payable} = 20,000 \times 20 = 400,000 \text{ yuan} \qquad (8-8)$$

8. 2. 4   Tax Incentive and Administration

8. 2. 4. 1   Exemption of Cultivated Land Occupation Tax

Farmland occupied by military facilities and farmland occupied by schools, kindergartens, social welfare institutions and medical institutions shall be exempted from the cultivated land occupation tax.

8. 2. 4. 2   Collection Management

The tax authorities shall be responsible for collecting the tax on the occupation of cultivated land. The tax liability of farmland occupation tax shall occur on the day when the taxpayer receives the written notice from the competent department of natural resources to handle the procedures for occupying cultivated land. The taxpayer shall declare and pay the farmland occupation tax within 30 days from the date of tax payment obligation.

8.3   Stamp Tax Law

Stamp tax is levied on the behavior of establishing books and receiving taxable certificates in economic activities and economic exchanges.

8. 3. 1   Taxpayers

The taxpayers of stamp duty are the units and individuals who establish, use and re-

ceive the certificates listed in the *Provisional Regulations of the People's Republic of China on Stamp Duty* (hereinafter referred to as *the Provisional Regulations on Stamp Duty*) within the territory of China, and shall perform their tax obligations according to the provisional regulations.

8.3.2 Tax Items and Tax Rates

8.3.2.1 Tax Items

The tax items of stamp tax refer to the items that should be paid in accordance with the *Provisional Regulations on Stamp Duty*. It specifically defines the scope of stamp tax. There are 13 items of stamp duty. There are two forms of stamp duty rate, namely the proportional tax rate and quota tax rate.

(1) Purchases and sales contract includes the contracts of supply, advance purchase, purchase, combination of purchase and sales and cooperation, adjustment, compensation, barter trade, etc. Tax shall be based on 0.3‰ of purchase and sales amount.

(2) Processing contract includes processing, customized, repairing, printing, advertising, surveying and mapping, testing and other contracts. Tax shall be based on 0.5‰ of the processing or contracting income.

(3) Contract for survey and design of construction projects includes survey and design contract. Tax shall be based on 0.5‰ of charge.

(4) Contract for construction and installation projects includes construction and installation contract. Tax shall be based on 0.3‰ of contract amount.

(5) Property leasing contract includes the contracts for the leasing of houses, ships, aircraft, motor vehicles, machinery, appliances and equipment, etc. Tax shall be based on 1‰ of the rental amount. If the tax amount is less than 1 yuan, it shall be pasted with 1 yuan.

(6) Contract of carriage of goods. Tax shall be based on 0.5‰ of transportation cost.

(7) Storage contract. Tax shall be based on 1‰ of storage cost.

(8) Loan contract. Tax shall be based on 0.05‰ of loan amount.

(9) Property insurance contract. Tax based on 1‰ of insurance premium.

(10) Technical contract includes contracts for technology development, transfer,

consultation and service, as well as documents used as contracts. Tax shall be based on 0. 3‰ of the recorded amount.

(11) Property transfer documents includes transfer documents of property ownership and copyright, exclusive right of trademark, patent right and the right to use proprietary technology, and rights transfer contracts such as patent implementation license contract, land use right transfer contract, commercial housing sales contract, etc. Tax shall be based on 0. 5‰ of the recorded amount.

(12) Business account books refer to the financial accounting books of an entity or individual recording production and operation activities. Tax shall be based on 0. 5‰ of the total amount of paid in capital and capital reserve. Other account books are taxed at 5 yuan per piece.

(13) Rights and licenses include housing ownership certificate, industrial and commercial business license, trademark registration certificate, patent certificate and land use certificate issued by government departments. Tax shall be based on 5 yuan for each license.

8. 3. 2. 2   Special Provisions on Tax Base

When the same voucher contains two or more economic items and different tax rates are applicable, if the amount is recorded separately, the tax payable shall be calculated separately, and the total tax amount shall be pasted after adding up. If the amount is not recorded separately, the tax shall be calculated at the higher tax rate.

When the taxable contract is signed, the tax liability has been generated, and the taxable amount shall be calculated and pasted. Therefore, no matter whether the contract is fulfilled or not, it should be taxed.

In the activities of purchasing and selling goods, the contract signed by means of exchanging goods for goods is a contract reflecting the dual economic behavior of both purchasing and selling. In this regard, the tax shall be calculated according to the total amount of purchase and sale specified in the contract.

8. 3. 3   Calculation of Tax Payable

The amount of tax payable by a taxpayer shall be calculated according to the nature of the tax payable certificate in terms of the proportion tax rate or fixed tax rate respectively.

• **Example 8-4**

An enterprise started business in February of a certain year, and the following business events occurred in the same year: one housing ownership certificate, one industrial and commercial business license, one land use certificate; one certificate of transfer of special technology use right with other enterprises, with the amount of 1 million yuan; one product purchase and sales contract, with the amount of 2 million yuan; and one loan contract, with the amount of 4 million yuan. Try to calculate the amount of stamp duty to be paid by the enterprise.

(1) The amount of tax payable according to the rights and licenses received by the enterprise:

$$\text{Tax Payable} = 3 \times 5 = 15 \text{ yuan} \tag{8-9}$$

(2) The amount of tax payable according to which the enterprise signs the transfer of property rights:

$$\text{Tax Payable} = 1,000,000 \times 0.5 \text{‰} = 500 \text{ yuan} \tag{8-10}$$

(3) The amount of tax payable in the purchases and sales contract concluded by the enterprise:

$$\text{Tax Payable} = 2,000,000 \times 0.3 \text{‰} = 600 \text{ yuan} \tag{8-11}$$

(4) The amount of tax payable when an enterprise enters into a loan contract:

$$\text{Tax Payable} = 4,000,000 \times 0.05 \text{‰} = 200 \text{ yuan} \tag{8-12}$$

(5) Total stamp duty payable by the enterprise in the current year:

$$15 + 500 + 600 + 200 = 1,315 \text{ yuan} \tag{8-13}$$

8.3.4 Tax Incentive

The tax reduction and exemption of stamp duty mainly includes several cases: ①Tax exemption for interest free and discount loan contracts; ②The leasing contracts signed by the real estate management department and individuals for living are exempt from stamp duty; ③Tax exemption for agricultural and animal husbandry insurance contracts.

8. 3. 5   The Administration

The stamp duty shall be applied when the book is established or received. It refers to the decal when the contract is signed, when the account book is opened and when the license is received.

Stamp duty is generally paid locally.

The taxpayers of stamp duty shall, in accordance with the relevant provisions of the regulations, timely file tax returns and truthfully fill in the stamp tax return form.

8. 4   Tobacco Tax Law

Tobacco tax is a kind of tax based on the amount of tobacco purchased by taxpayers.

8. 4. 1   Taxpayers and Scope of Taxation

8. 4. 1. 1   Taxpayers

Within the territory of the People's Republic of China, the units that purchase tobacco leaf in accordance with the provisions of the *Law of the People's Republic of China on Tobacco Monopoly* are the taxpayers of tobacco tax.

8. 4. 1. 2   Scope of Taxation

The tax scope of tobacco leaf tax refers to air dried tobacco leaves and flue-cured tobacco leaves.

8. 4. 1. 3   Tax Base

The tax base of tobacco tax is the total price actually paid by taxpayers for purchasing tobacco leaves.

8.4.2　Tax Rate and Calculation of Tax Payable

8.4.2.1　Tax Rate

The tobacco leaf tax rate is 20%.

8.4.2.2　Calculation of Tax Payable

The taxable amount of tobacco tax shall be calculated by multiplying the total amount of the price actually paid by the taxpayer for purchasing tobacco leaf by the tax rate, and the calculation formula is as follows:

$$\text{Tax Payable} = \text{Actual Payment} \times \text{Tax Rate} \qquad (8\text{-}14)$$

The total price actually paid by taxpayers for purchasing tobacco leaves includes the purchase price and extra price subsidies paid by taxpayers to tobacco production and sales units and individuals. The extra price subsidy is calculated by 10% of the purchase price of tobacco.

$$\text{Actual Payment} = \text{Purchase Amount} \times (1 + 10\%) \qquad (8\text{-}15)$$

- **Example　8-5**

A tobacco company is a general VAT taxpayer. In January 2019, it purchased 100,000 kg of tobacco leaf, with a purchase price of 10 yuan/kg, totaling 1,000,000 yuan, and the payment has been made in full. Please calculate the tobacco tax that the tobacco company should pay when purchasing tobacco in August.

$$\text{Tobacco Tax Payable} = 1,000,000 \times (1 + 10\%) \times 20\% = 220,000 \text{ yuan}$$

$$(8\text{-}16)$$

8.4.3　The Administration

The collection and administration of tobacco tax shall be implemented in accordance with the relevant provisions of the *Law of the People's Republic of China on the Administration of Tax Collection* and the *Law of the People's Republic of China on Tobacco Monopoly*.

The time when the tax liability of tobacco tax occurs is the day when the taxpayer purchases the tobacco leaf. The date of purchasing tobacco leaf refers to the day on which the taxpayer pays off the purchase money or issues the certificate of purchasing tobacco leaf to the tobacco seller.

　　When purchasing tobacco leaves, a taxpayer shall declare and pay tobacco tax to the competent tax authorities in the place where the tobacco leaves are purchased.

　　Tobacco tax shall be calculated and collected monthly, and the taxpayer shall declare and pay the tax within 15 days from the end of the month in which the tax payment obligation occurs.

8.5　Vessel Tonnage Tax Law

　　Vessel Tonnage Tax (short for VTT) is levied on the taxable ships according to the carrying capacity when the taxable ships entering the domestic ports from ports outside the territory of the People's Republic of China. Vessel Tonnage Tax is collected and administrated by China Customs. The basic norm is the *Vessel Tonnage Tax Law of the People's Republic of the China*, which was implemented on July 1, 2018.

8.5.1　Scope of Taxation and Tax Rates

8.5.1.1　Scope of Taxation

　　Ships entering domestic ports from foreign ports of the People's Republic of China (hereinafter referred to as "taxable ships") shall pay tonnage tax (hereinafter referred to as ton tax). The tax items and tax rates of ton tax shall be implemented in accordance with the table of tax items and tax rates of ton tax.

8.5.1.2　Tax Rates

　　Preferential tax rate and ordinary tax rate are set for ton tax. For taxable ships of the nationality of the People's Republic of China, the preferential tax rate shall be applicable to the taxable ships with the nationality of the People's Republic of China, where the country (region) of the ship's nationality and the People's Republic of China have signed a treaty or agreement containing the most favored nation treatment for ship taxes and fees. Other taxable ships are subject to the general tax rate. Table 8−1 shows the list of vessel tonnage tax items and rates.

Table 8-1   List of Vessel Tonnage Tax Items and Rates

The net tonnage of taxable vessels	Unit tax rates (yuan per net tonnage)					
	Ordinary tax rates (Divided by the period of the applicable licenses)			Preferential tax rates (Divided by the period of the applicable licenses)		
	1 year	90 days	30 days	1 year	90 days	30 days
Not more than 2, 000 tonnages	12. 6	4. 2	2. 1	9. 0	3. 0	1. 5
More than 2, 000 tonnages, but not more than 10, 000 tonnages	24. 0	8. 0	4. 0	17. 4	5. 8	2. 9
More than 10, 000 tonnages, but not more than 50, 000 tonnages	27. 6	9. 2	4. 6	19. 8	6. 6	3. 3
More than 50, 000 tonnages	31. 8	10. 6	5. 3	22. 8	7. 6	3. 8

Data source: The data is summarized from the *Tax Law* (2021) textbook for the Chinese CPA Examination organized by the CICPA.

8.5.2   Calculation of Tax Payable

The vessel tonnage tax is levied according to the net tonnage of the ship and the period of the tonnage tax license, and the calculation formula is as follows:

$$\text{Tax Payable} = \text{Net Tonnage of Ship} \times \text{Fixed Tax Rate} \qquad (8-17)$$

The customs shall be responsible for collecting the tonnage tax. When levying ton tax, the customs shall prepare and issue payment certificates. After the person in charge of the dutiable ship has paid the tonnage tax or provided a guarantee, the customs shall fill in and issue the tonnage tax license according to the period of the license applied for.

• Example 8-6

A cargo ship of a transport company in country B sails into a port in China, and the net tonnage of the cargo ship is 30, 000 tons. The person in charge of the cargo ship has obtained the tonnage tax license from the Customs of China, and the period of stay in the port is 30 days. Country B has signed a clause on the reciprocal most favored nation treatment of ship taxes and fees with China. Please calculate the tonnage tax that the person in charge of the cargo ship should pay to our customs.

(1) According to the relevant provisions of ship tonnage tax, the freighter shall enjoy preferential tax rate of RMB 3. 3 per net tonnage.

(2) Ship tonnage tax payable = 30, 000×3. 3 = 99, 000 yuan.

8. 5. 3 Tax Incentive and Administration

Except for military vessels, police vessels, non-motorized vessels, fishing vessels and ships with a taxable amount of less than ¥ 50, all other commercial vessels are required to pay the vessel Tonnage Tax.

The tonnage tax shall be paid and obtain the license of vessel tonnage tax when the taxable ship eatering anyone port of China. And when the taxable ship leave the port, the license of vessel Tonnage Tax shall be sumbitted. If a taxable vessel has not left the port after the expiration of the license, it shall apply for a new license and repay the tonnage tax.

Chapter

9

International Taxation and
Tax Administration

With the increasingly frequent and in-depth development of international exchanges, international tax issues are also increasing.

Tax treaties reflect the collective efforts of different countries to reduce double taxation across borders. Base erosion and profit shifting (BEPS) reflects the collective efforts of the tax authority community around the globe to mitigate and rein in tax avoidance.

9.1   International Taxation

9.1.1   Tax Jurisdiction

International taxation refers to the taxation distribution between two or more sovereign states or regions, based on their respective taxation sovereignty, in the collection and payment relationship formed by levying taxes separately on transnational taxpayers.

A series of contradictions in the relation of international tax distribution are all related to tax jurisdiction. Generally according to the internationally recognized order, there are two principles of jurisdiction of taxation, namely source jurisdiction and residence jurisdiction. The source jurisdiction is based on the source of taxpayers' income or the location of economic activities. The residence jurisdiction is based on the taxpayer's nationality and domicile.

9.1.2   International Double Taxation

International double taxation, also known as international double taxation, refers to the overlapping taxation formed by two or more countries levying separately on the same target of the same transnational taxpayer.

From a practical point of view, as the root cause of international double taxation, the relevant countries exercise the source jurisdiction and residence jurisdiction over the same income of the same transnational taxpayer at the same time, resulting in the overlapping of tax jurisdiction. Due to the unavoidable situation of transnational income and the long-term existence of various international tax jurisdictions, the problem of international double taxation will be prevalent in the international tax activities for a long time.

9.1.3 Tax Treaties

Tax treaties are also called double tax agreements or DTAs. Many countries have entered into tax treaties with other countries in order to avoid or mitigate double taxation. One exception is tax havens, which are generally offshore countries that offer foreign individuals and businesses little or no tax liability. These countries typically do not enter into tax treaties.

Tax treaties may cover a range of taxes including income taxes, inheritance taxes, value added taxes, or other taxes. Besides bilateral treaties, multilateral treaties are also in place, which means more than two countries can be involved.

All tax treaties are different and very few are alike. However, most treaties share some common elements that are worth noticing.

(1) Tax treaties define which taxes are covered and who is a resident and eligible for benefits.

(2) Tax treaties reduce the amounts of tax withheld from interest, dividends, and royalties paid by a resident of one country to residents of the other country.

(3) Tax treaties limit tax of one country on business income of a resident of the other country to that income from a permanent establishment in the first country.

(4) Tax treaties define circumstances in which income of individuals resident in one country will be taxed in the other country, including salary, self-employment, pension, and other income.

(5) Tax treaties provide for exemption of certain types of organizations or individuals, and provide procedural frameworks for enforcement and dispute resolution.

(6) The stated goals for entering into a treaty usually include reduction of double taxation, eliminating tax evasion, and encouraging cross-border trade efficiency.

(7) It is generally accepted that tax treaties improve certainty for taxpayers and tax au-

thorities in their international dealings.

9.1.4   International Anti-tax Avoidance and Tax Cooperation

International tax avoidance is not only a simple matter of perfecting tax laws and tax agreements and ensuring the tax revenue of relevant countries. Moreover, it involves international and national economic efficiency and social equity, affects the tax interests of relevant countries, and distorts the tax distribution relationship between countries. Therefore, governments and the international community should not only take measures to avoid the international double taxation of income, but also take measures to prevent the international tax avoidance of transnational taxpayers.

International tax avoidance refers to the behavior of taxpayers to evade or mitigate their total global tax obligations by taking advantage of loopholes, exceptions and defects in tax laws of two or more countries and tax agreements between countries.

In real life, transnational taxpayers can migrate to avoid tax jurisdiction and realize international tax avoidance by moving out or falsely moving out or not moving out of high-tax countries. In order to avoid international double taxation, countries should use of national or international tax agreements to avoid tax avoidance.

Base erosion and profit shifting refers to tax planning strategies used by multinational enterprises (MNEs) that exploit gaps and mismatches in tax rules to avoid paying tax. BEPS project, on the other hand, is an OECD/G20 project to set up an inclusive international framework to combat tax avoidance by multinational enterprises using base erosion and profit shifting tools. It is estimated that BEPS practices cost countries USD 100-240 billion in lost revenue annually. The BEPS project is led by the OECD's Committee on Fiscal Affairs, and began in 2013 with OECD and G20 countries in a context of financial crisis. After the BEPS report has been delivered in 2015, the project is now in its implementation phase, more than 130 countries and jurisdictions are involved, including a majority of developing countries.

The BEPS project looks to develop multilateral dialogue and could be achieved thanks to a successful international cooperation. It is one of the instances of the OECD that involves developing countries in its process.

As a direct result of such large-scale international collaboration, the BEPS Package provides 15 Actions that equip governments with the domestic and international instruments needed to tackle tax avoidance. Countries now have the tools to ensure that profits are taxed where profits-generating economic activities are performed and where value is created. Moreover, OECD and G20 countries along with developing countries that are participating in the implementation of the BEPS Package and the ongoing development of anti-BEPS international standards are truly establishing a modern and international tax framework to ensure profits are taxed where economic activity and value creation occur.

The BEPS project consists of 15 Actions with 4 of them minimum standards, agreed to by all participating countries who have committed to consistent implementation.

(1) Action 1: Address the digital economy. As the whole world is witnessing the surge of digital economy in recent decade, the BEPS project recommends avoiding new direct taxes on digital activity, and expects other actions to be generalized to tackle the digital economy as well. For indirect taxes, a shift to tax collection in the jurisdiction of consumption is recommended. This action also paves the way for more taxes to be collected on low-value e-commerce transactions by shifting value-added tax obligations to the vendor.

(2) Action 2: Hybrids. This action advises the creation of domestic mismatching rules, which addresses the different treatment of corporate taxable activity by nations. It also commends tax treaty provisions that eliminate issues like double non-taxation or double deduction.

(3) Action 3: Controlled Foreign Companies (CFCs) Rules. This action seeks to establish a standard definition of a CFC and its income, and proposes rules that eliminate mismatches or loopholes that allow CFCs to shift income elsewhere.

(4) Action 4: Interest deductions. This action outlines a common approach to end base erosion by interest deduction rules for eligible MNEs. It also suggests rules that account for a firm's debt level and interest deductions, creating a ratio standard that prevents MNEs from favorable tax deductions.

(5) Action 5: Harmful tax practices. This action is one of the four minimum standards. Which means if a country chooses to commit to the BEPS project, it must commit to at least this action and other three minimum standards. This action allows for a methodology that assesses harmful tax practices, like preferential regimes. It also creates a framework for compulsory spontaneous exchange of information regarding tax rulings and practices.

(6) Action 6: Treaty abuse, which is also a minimum standard. This action creates

several provisions for a minimum standard to combat treaty shopping that all participating countries have agreed to implement. It also suggests specific anti-abuse rules be included in domestic legislation.

（7）Action 7: Permanent establishment status. This action greatly expands the definition of a permanent establishment to counter MNEs tactics used to avoid having a taxable presence in a country.

（8）Actions 8-10: Transfer pricing. It is a very complicated and interesting issue on the cutting-edge international taxation practice. But we don't have the time to go into detail.

In general, these actions move to align transfer pricing outcomes with actual value creation. And they also create stronger guidelines to transactions involving the transfer pricing of intangibles and contractual arrangements.

（9）Action 11: BEPS data analysis. This action establishes the synchronization of data collection, which indicators to look to, and methodologies to analyze data with.

（10）Action 12: Disclosure of aggressive tax planning. This action recommends mandatory disclosure of aggressive tax planning to increase transparency.

（11）Action 13: Transfer pricing documentation, which is the third minimum standard. It provides guidelines for documentation of transfer pricing, including country-to-country disclosure.

（12）Action 14: Dispute resolution, which is the last minimum standard. It stipulates minimum standards for treaty disputes and arbitration.

（13）Action 15: Multilateral instrument. This action lays out the legal and technical difficulties the BEPS project faces in its mission to create a multilateral tax framework. The instrument is called "Multilateral Convention to Implement Tax Treaty Related Measures to Prevent Base Erosion and Profit Shifting" and entered into force on 1st July 2018.

9.2 Tax Administration

The Law of the People's Republic of China on the Administration of Tax Collection is the general term of the laws and regulations related to tax collection management, including tax collection management law and relevant laws, regulations and rules of tax collection management.

9. 2. 1　Overview

9. 2. 1. 1　The Legislative Purpose of Tax Collection Management Law

Article 1 of the *Law of the People's Republic of China on the Administration of Tax Collection* stipulates: "this law is formulated in order to strengthen the administration of tax collection, standardize the behavior of tax collection and payment, safeguard the state's tax revenue, protect the legitimate rights and interests of taxpayers, and promote economic and social development. "

9. 2. 1. 2　The Applicable Scope of tax collection and Administration Law

Article 2 of the *Law of the People's Republic of China on the Administration of Tax Collection* stipulates: "this law shall apply to the administration of the collection of various taxes collected by the tax authorities in accordance with the law. " This clearly defines the scope of application of the tax collection and management law.

China's tax collection agencies include the tax and customs departments. The tax authorities collect various industrial and commercial taxes, and the customs collects customs duties. The *Law of the People's Republic of China on the Administration of Tax Collection* is only applicable to the collection and management of various taxes collected by tax authorities. Other laws and regulations shall apply to the customs duties, value-added tax and consumption tax levied by the customs.

9. 2. 2　Tax Registration Management

Tax registration, also known as tax registration, is the primary link and basic work for tax authorities to implement tax administration on taxpayers. It is the basis and proof for the establishment of the legal relationship between the two sides, and it is also the obligation that taxpayers must perform according to law.

Enterprises, branches set up by enterprises in other places and places engaged in production and business operations, individual businesses and institutions engaged in production and business operations shall go through tax registration.

In addition to state organs, individuals and mobile rural hawkers without fixed production and business places, other taxpayers shall also go through tax registration. According to the provisions of tax laws and administrative regulations, withholding agents (except state organs) who have the obligation of withholding tax shall register the withholding tax in accordance with the provisions.

The tax bureau implements the unified taxpayer identification number. The taxpayer identification number is unique.

When handling the following matters, a taxpayer must provide a tax registration certificate, by opening a bank account, collecting and purchasing invoices.

According to the tax administration law and the administrative measures for tax registration issued by the State Taxation Administration, China's tax registration system generally includes the following contents:

9. 2. 2. 1   Establishment of Tax Registration

Enterprises, branches set up by enterprises in other places and places engaged in production and business operations, individual businesses and institutions engaged in production and business operations (hereinafter referred to as "taxpayers engaged in production and business operations") shall report to the local tax authorities for tax registration.

9. 2. 2. 2   Change and Cancellation of Tax Registration

The change of tax registration refers to the tax registration procedures that the taxpayer reports to the tax authority when the content of the tax registration changes; the cancellation of the tax registration refers to the tax registration procedures that the taxpayer applies to the tax authority for handling when the taxpayer's tax registration content has changed fundamentally and needs to terminate the performance of tax payment obligations according to law.

9. 2. 3   Account Book and Voucher Management

Account book is the book of accounts or the book that the taxpayer and withholding agent continuously record their various economic business. The voucher is a written certificate used by taxpayers to record economic business, clarify economic responsibility and register account books.

9. 2. 3. 1 Management of Account Book and Voucher Settings

Account sets the range of account books. All taxpayers and withholding agents must set up account books in accordance with relevant laws, administrative regulations and the provisions of the financial and tax authorities under the State Council.

A taxpayer engaged in production or business operations shall set up account books within 15 days from the date of receipt of business license or occurrence of tax liability.

According to Article 24 of the *Law of the People's Republic of China on the Administration of Tax Collection*, taxpayers and withholding agents engaged in production and business operations must keep account books, accounting vouchers, tax payment vouchers and other relevant materials within the storage period stipulated by the competent financial and tax authorities of the State Council. Account books, accounting vouchers, statements, tax payment certificates, invoices, export vouchers and other relevant tax related materials shall not be forged, altered or damaged without authorization.

Unless otherwise specified, account books, accounting vouchers, statements, tax payment certificates, invoices, export vouchers and other relevant tax related materials shall be kept for 10 years.

9. 2. 3. 2 Invoice Management

According to Article 21 of the *Law of the People's Republic of China on the Administration of Tax Collection*, "tax authorities are the competent authorities of invoices and are responsible for the management and supervision of printing, purchasing, issuing, obtaining, keeping, handing in and cancellation of invoices."

The basic form of invoice includes stub, invoice and bookkeeping. The counterfoil copy shall be kept by the payee or the drawer for future reference; the invoice form shall be used as the original payment voucher by the payer or the drawee; the bookkeeping copy shall be the original bookkeeping voucher by the payee or the drawer.

Units and individuals who have gone through tax registration according to law shall apply to the competent tax authorities for receiving and purchasing invoices after receiving the tax registration certificate.

Taxpayers can apply for receiving ordinary invoices according to their own needs. VAT special invoice is only used by general VAT taxpayers.

Management of invoice issuing, using and obtaining. According to Article 21 of the *Law of the People's Republic of China on the Administration of Tax Collection*, "units and individuals shall issue, use and obtain invoices in accordance with regulations when purchasing and selling commodities, providing or accepting business services and engaging in other business activities. "

The units and individuals that issue invoices shall storeand keep them in accordance with relevant regulations. The invoice counterfoil and invoice register shall be kept for five years. After the expiration of the storage period, it shall be reported to the tax authorities for inspection and destruction.

If a taxpayer has the obligation of tax declaration, but has not made any tax declaration for three consecutive months, the tax collection and management system will automatically identify the taxpayer as an abnormal household and stop using the invoice collection book and invoice.

The tax authorities shall, in accordance with the Tax collection and Administration law, pursue the collection of taxes and late payment fines for non-normal households who owe taxes.

9. 2. 3. 3   Tax Declaration Management

Article 23 of the *Law of the People's Republic of China on the Administration of Tax Collection* stipulates that "the State shall actively promote the use of tax control devices in accordance with the needs of tax collection and management. Taxpayers shall install and use tax control devices in accordance with regulations, and shall not damage or alter tax control devices without authorization. " According to Article 60 of the *Low of the People's Republic of China on the Administration of Tax Collection*, those who are unable to install or use tax control devices in accordance with regulations, damage or alter tax control devices without authorization shall be ordered by the tax authorities to make corrections within a time limit and may be fined not more than 2, 000 yuan; if the circumstances are serious, a fine of not less than 2, 000 yuan but not more than 10, 000 yuan shall be imposed.

According to Article 25 of the *Law of the People's Republic of China on the Administration of Tax Collection*, the objects of tax declaration are taxpayers and withholding agents. If there is no tax payable within the tax period, the taxpayer shall also file a tax return in accordance with the provisions.

9.3   Tax Collection

9.3.1   Principles of Tax Collection

According to Article 29 of the *Law of the People's Republic of China on the Administration of Tax Collection*, no unit or individual shall collect tax except tax authorities, tax personnel and units and individuals entrusted by tax authorities in accordance with laws and administrative regulations.

According to Article 28 of the *Law of the People's Republic of China on the Administration of Tax Collection*, tax authorities can only collect taxes in accordance with laws and administrative regulations. Without the adjustment of legal organs and legal procedures, both sides of levy and payment shall not change at will. Tax authorities, on behalf of the state, collect taxes from taxpayers, which cannot be collected arbitrarily, but can only be collected according to law.

In the process of tax collection, tax authorities shall collect taxes in accordance with the tax collection standards prescribed in advance by tax laws and administrative regulations. It is not allowed to increase or change tax items, increase or reduce tax rates, increase or reduce taxes, collect or delay the collection of taxes in advance, and apportion taxes without authorization.

Tax authorities must abide by the legal authority and procedures in collecting taxes. When levying taxes or seizing or sealing up commodities, goods or other property, the tax authorities must issue tax payment certificates to taxpayers or issue receipts or checklists for seizure or sealing up. Taxes, overdue fines and fines shall be turned over to the state treasury by the tax authorities.

According to Article 45 of the *Law of the People's Republic of China on the Administration of Tax Collection*, for the first time, the priority of tax is determined in law, and the order of tax collection is determined when the taxpayer pays various payments and repays debts.

(1) Tax has priority over unsecured claims.

(2) If the taxpayer owes more taxes, the tax shall be prior to the execution of mortgage, pledge and lien.

(3) Tax has priority over fine and confiscation of illegal income.

9. 3. 2   Tax Collection System

9. 3. 2. 1   System of Withholding, Remitting and Collecting Taxes

(1) The tax authorities shall not require the units and individuals that are not required by laws and administrative regulations to perform the duty of withholding or collecting taxes.

(2) The withholding agent stipulated in the tax law must perform the duty of withholding and collecting tax according to law. If you don't fulfill your obligations, you have to bear legal responsibility. In addition to being punished in accordance with the provisional of the *Law of the People's Republic of China on the Administration of Tax Collection* and the detailed rules for implementation, the withholding agent shall be required to make up for the amount of tax that should be withheld or collected within a specified period of time.

(3) When the withholding agent performs the duty of withholding and collecting tax according to law, the taxpayer shall not refuse.

(4) The tax authorities shall pay the withholding agent handling fees for withholding and collecting in accordance with the regulations.

9. 3. 2. 2   Collection System of Tax Overdue Fine

Article 32 of the *Law of the People's Republic of China on the Administration of Tax Collection* stipulates: "If a taxpayer fails to pay tax within the prescribed time limit, and the withholding agent fails to hand over the tax within the prescribed time limit, the tax authorities shall, in addition to ordering the payment within a specified time limit, impose an additional fine of 0. 05% of the overdue tax per day from the date of overdue payment."

9. 3. 2. 3   Tax Protection Measures

Tax preservation measures refer to the measures taken by tax authorities to restrict taxpayers to handle or transfer commodities, goods or other properties in cases where the tax collection cannot be guaranteed due to the taxpayer's behavior or some objective reasons.

9. 3. 2. 4　Tax Enforcement Measures

Compulsory tax enforcement measures refer to the behavior that the parties concerned fail to perform their obligations stipulated by laws and administrative regulations, and the relevant state organs use legal compulsory means to force the parties to perform their obligations.

Article 40 of the *Law of the People's Republic of China on the Administration of Tax Collection* stipulates that if a taxpayer engaged in production or business operations or a withholding agent fails to pay or remit tax within the prescribed time limit, and a tax payment guarantor fails to pay the guaranteed tax within the prescribed time limit, the tax authorities shall order the taxpayer to pay within a specified time limit. If the taxpayer fails to pay the tax within the prescribed time limit, the tax authorities may take compulsory enforcement measures with the approval of the director of the tax bureau at or above the county level measures.

9. 3. 2. 5　Tax Refund and Recovery System

(1) Refund of tax. Article 51 of the *Law of the People's Republic of China on the Administration of Tax Collection* stipulates that the tax paid by a taxpayer in excess of the amount of tax payable shall be refunded immediately after it is discovered by the tax authorities; if a taxpayer finds out within three years from the date of settlement and payment of tax, he/she may ask the tax authorities to refund the overpaid tax and calculate the bank deposit interest for the same period, and the tax authorities shall refund it immediately after timely verification.

(2) Tax collection. Article 52 of the *Law of the People's Republic of China on the Administration of Tax Collection* stipulates: "If a taxpayer or withholding agent fails to pay or underpayments tax due to the responsibility of the tax authorities, the tax authorities may, within three years, require the taxpayer or withholding agent to make up the tax payment, but shall not impose any overdue fine."

If the taxpayer or withholding agent fails to pay or underpays the tax due to calculation errors of the taxpayer or withholding agent, the tax authorities may pursue the collection of tax and overdue fine within three years; if there are special circumstances, the period of recovery may be extended to five years.

The term "special circumstances" refers to the fact that a taxpayer or withholding agent fails to pay or underpayments, or fails to deduct or collect less taxes due to errors in calculation and other errors, with an accumulated amount of more than 100, 000 yuan.

In the case of tax evasion, refusal to pay or tax fraud, the tax authorities shall not be subject to the time limit prescribed in the preceding paragraph in pursuing the amount of tax that has not been paid or underpaid, the fine for overdue payment or the tax defrauded.

9. 4   Tax Inspection

9. 4. 1   Key Inspection

Key inspection refers to the inspection of taxpayers who have tax evasion or suspicion of tax evasion, which are reported by citizens, handed over by higher authorities or transferred by relevant departments, whose tax declaration is obviously inconsistent with the actual production and operation situation, and industries with general tax evasion.

9. 4. 2   Classification Plan Inspection

Classified planned inspection refers to the inspection conducted according to the taxpayer's historical tax situation, taxpayer's scale of tax payment and the length of tax inspection interval, according to the taxpayer's classification, planned inspection time and inspection frequency.

9. 4. 3   Centralized Inspection

Centralized inspection refers to the tax inspection uniformly arranged and organized by the tax authorities within a certain period of time and within a certain scope. This kind of inspection is generally large-scale, such as the national tax and financial inspection in the previous years.

9. 4. 4　Temporary Inspection

Temporary inspection refers to the inspection arranged outside the normal inspection plan by tax authorities at all levels according to different economic situation, tax evasion trend, completion of tax tasks and other comprehensive factors, such as professional anatomy, typical investigation examination and so on.

9. 4. 5　Special Inspection

Special inspection refers to the inspection of a certain tax type or a certain link of tax collection management conducted by the tax authorities according to the actual tax work, for example, the general special inspection of VAT payment, the special inspection of tax evasion and so on.

9. 5　Legal Liability

(1) According to Article 60 of the *Law of the People's Republic of China on the Administration of Tax Collection* and Article 90 of the detailed rules for implementation, if a taxpayer commits one of the following acts, it shall be ordered by the tax authorities to make corrections within a time limit, and may be fined not more than 2, 000 yuan but not more than 10, 000 yuan if the circumstances are serious. ①Failing to apply for tax registration, alteration or cancellation of registration within the prescribed time limit; ②Failing to set up and keep account books or keep accounting vouchers and relevant materials in accordance with regulations; ③Failing to submit the financial and accounting systems, financial and accounting treatment methods and accounting software to the tax authorities for reference in accordance with the provisions; ④Failing to report all the bank accounts to the tax authorities in accordance with the provisions; ⑤Failing to install or use tax control devices in accordance with regulations, or damaging or altering tax control devices without authorization; ⑥Failing to go through the procedures of verifying or replacing the tax registration certificate

in accordance with the provisions.

(2) If a taxpayer fails to go through tax registration, it shall be ordered by the tax authorities to make corrections within a time limit; if the taxpayer fails to do so within the time limit, its business license shall be revoked by the administrative department for industry and commerce.

(3) If a taxpayer fraudulently obtains the tax registration certificate by providing false proof materials, he shall be fined not more than 2, 000 yuan; if the circumstances are serious, he shall be fined not less than 2, 000 yuan but not more than 10, 000 yuan.

(4) If the withholding agent fails to register the withholding tax in accordance with the provisions, the tax authorities shall order the withholding agent to make corrections within a time limit within three days from the date of discovery, and may also impose a fine of less than 1, 000 yuan.

(5) Article 61 of the *Law of the People's Republic of China on the Administration of Tax Collection* stipulates: "If a withholding agent fails to establish and preserve account books for the tax withheld and remitted or tax collected and remitted, or keep the vouchers for the accounts and relevant information regarding the tax withholding and remitted or tax collected and remitted, in accordance with relevant regulations, it shall be ordered by the tax authorities to rectify within a time limit and may be fined not more than 2, 000 yuan; if the circumstances are serious, it shall be fined not less than 2, 000 yuan but not more than 5, 000 yuan. "

(6) Article 62 of the *Law of the People's Republic of China on the Administration of Tax Collection* stipulates: "If a taxpayer fails to file tax returns and submit tax information within the prescribed time limit, or if a withholding agent fails to submit a tax withholding or collection and payment report and relevant materials to the tax authorities within the prescribed time limit, the tax authorities shall order it to make corrections within a time limit and may impose a fine of less than 2, 000 yuan; if the circumstances are serious, it may be punished with a fine of less than 2, 000 yuan A fine of not less than 1, 000 yuan but not more than 10, 000 yuan. "

(7) Identification of tax evasion and its legal liability. Article 63 of the *Law of the People's Republic of China on the Administration of Tax Collection* stipulates that "taxpayers, who forge, alter, conceal or destroy account books and accounting vouchers without authorization, or overstate expenditures and fail to list income or list less income in the account

books, or refuse to declare or make false tax returns after being informed by the tax authorities, and fail to pay or underpay the tax payable, conduct tax evasion. If a taxpayer evades tax, the tax authorities shall pursue the payment of the tax they fail to pay or underpaid and the overdue fine, and impose a fine of not less than 50% but not more than five times the amount of tax not paid or underpaid; if a crime is constituted, the offender shall be investigated for criminal responsibility according to law. If a withholding agent fails to pay or underpays the tax withheld or collected by means of the means mentioned in the preceding paragraph, the tax authorities shall recover the tax not paid or underpaid and the fine for overdue payment, and shall also impose a fine of not less than 50% but not more than five times the amount of tax not paid or underpaid; if a crime is constituted, the offender shall be investigated for criminal responsibility according to law. "

(8) Article 201 of the *Criminal Law of the People's Republic of China* (hereinafter referred to as *the Criminal Law*) stipulates that if a taxpayer makes false tax declaration or fails to declare tax by deception or concealment, and evades paying more than 10% of the tax payable, he or she shall be sentenced to fixed-term imprisonment of not more than three years or criminal detention and shall also be fined. If the amount is huge and accounts for more than 30% of the tax payable, he or she shall be sentenced to 3 fixed-term imprisonment of not less than three years but not more than seven years and shall also be fined.

(9) Legal liability for false declaration or non-declaration. Article 64 of the *Law of the People's Republic of China on the Administration of Tax Collection* stipulates: "If a taxpayer or withholding agent fabricates a false basis for tax calculation, the tax authorities shall order it to make corrections within a time limit and impose a fine of less than 50, 000 yuan.

If a taxpayer fails to file a tax return or fails to pay or underpay the tax payable, the tax authorities shall pursue the payment of the tax not paid or underpaid and the overdue fine, and shall also impose a fine of not less than 50% but not more than five times the amount of tax not paid or underpaid. "

(10) The legal responsibility of evading the recovery of overdue taxes. Article 65 of the *Law of the People's Republic of China on the Administration of Tax Collection* stipulates: "If a taxpayer fails to pay the tax payable and obstructs the tax authorities from pursuing the overdue tax by means of transferring or concealing his property, the tax authorities shall pursue the overdue tax and overdue fine, and impose a fine of 50% to 5 times of the tax in arrears. If a crime is constituted, the offender shall be investigated for criminal responsibility

in accordance with the law. "

Article 203 of *the Criminal Law* stipulates: "If a taxpayer fails to pay the tax payable and takes the means of transferring or concealing his property, which makes it impossible for the tax authorities to recover the overdue tax, if the amount is between 10, 000 yuan and 100, 000 yuan, he or she shall be sentenced to fixed-term imprisonment of not more than three years or criminal detention, and shall also, or shall only, be fined not less than one time but not more than five times the amount of tax in arrears. If the amount is more than 100, 000 yuan, he or she shall be sentenced to not less than three years but not more than seven years, and shall also be fined not less than one time but not more than five times the a-mount of tax not paid. "

(11) Legal liability of defrauding export tax rebate. Article 66 of the *Law of the People's Republic of China on the Administration of Tax Collection* stipulates that "if a person fraudulently obtains the state's export tax refund by false declaration of export or by other deceptive means, the tax authorities shall pursue the tax refund and impose a fine of not less than one time but not more than five times the amount of tax defrauded. If a crime is consti-tuted, the offender shall be investigated for criminal responsibility in accordance with the law. "

The tax authorities may, within the prescribed period, stop handling export tax refund for those who cheat the state for export tax refund.

Article 204 of *the Criminal Law* stipulates: "Anyone who fraudulently obtains tax refund from the state for export by false declaration of export or other deceptive means, if the amount is relatively large, shall be sentenced to fixed-term imprisonment of not more than five years or criminal detention and shall also be fined not less than one time but not more than five times the amount of tax defrauded. If the amount is huge or there are other serious circum-stances, he or she shall be sentenced to fixed-term imprisonment of not less than five years but not more than 10 years and shall also be fined not less than one time but not more than five times the amount defrauded. If the amount is especially huge or there are other especially serious circumstances, he or she shall be sentenced to fixed-term imprisonment of not less than 10 years or life imprisonment and shall also be fined not less than one time but not more than five times the amount of tax defrauded or be sentenced to confiscation of property. "

(12) The legal responsibility of tax resistance. Article 67 of the *Law of the People's Republic of China on the Administration of Tax Collection* stipulates that "those who refuse to

pay taxes by means of violence or threat are tax resisters. In addition to the tax authorities' recovery of the tax they refuse to pay and the overdue fine, the offender shall be investigated for criminal responsibility in accordance with the law. If the circumstances are not serious enough to constitute a crime, the tax authorities shall pursue the payment of the tax they refuse to pay and the fine for overdue payment and impose a fine of not less than one time but not more than five times the amount of tax refused. "

Article 202 of *the Criminal Law* stipulates: "Whoever refuses to pay taxes by means of violence or threat shall be sentenced to fixed-term imprisonment of not more than three years or criminal detention and shall also be fined not less than one time but not more than five times the amount of tax he refuses to pay. If the circumstances are serious, he or she shall be sentenced to fixed-term imprisonment of not less than three years but not more than seven years and shall also be fined not less than one time but not more than five times the amount of tax he refuses to pay. "

(13) Legal liability for failing to pay or underpaying taxes within the prescribed time limit. Article 68 of the *Law of the People's Republic of China on the Administration of Tax Collection* stipulates: "If a taxpayer or withholding agent fails to pay or underpayments the amount of tax that should be paid or remitted within the prescribed time limit and is ordered by the tax authorities to pay within a specified time limit, the tax authorities may, in addition to taking enforcement measures in accordance with the provisions of Article 40 of this law, recover the tax not paid or underpaid by a fine of more than 50% but less than five times the amount of the tax. "

(14) Legal liability of withholding agent for not performing withholding obligation. Article 69 of the *Law of the People's Republic of China on the Administration of Tax Collection* stipulates that "if a withholding agent fails to collect tax due to withholding or receivable, the tax authorities shall recover the tax from the taxpayer and impose a fine of more than 50% and less than three times the amount of tax that should be withheld or receivable. "

(15) The legal responsibility of failing to cooperate with the tax authorities in the inspection according to law. Article 70 of the *Law of the People's Republic of China on the Administration of Tax Collection* stipulates: "If a taxpayer or withholding agent evades, refuses or obstructs the inspection of the tax authorities in other ways, the tax authorities shall order it to make corrections and may impose a fine of less than 10, 000 yuan. If the circumstances are serious, a fine of not less than 10, 000 yuan but not more than 50, 000 yuan shall be

imposed. "

(16) Legal liability of illegal printing of invoice. Article 71 of the *Law of the People's Republic of China on the Administration of Tax Collection* stipulates: "In case of illegal printing of invoices in violation of the provisions of Article 22 of this law, the tax authorities shall destroy the illegally printed invoices, confiscate the illegal income and tools of crime, and impose a fine of not less than 10, 000 yuan but not more than 50, 000 yuan. If a crime is constituted, criminal responsibility shall be investigated in accordance with the law. "

Article 206 of *the Criminal Law* stipulates: "Whoever forges or sells forged special invoices for value-added tax shall be sentenced to fixed-term imprisonment of not more than three years, criminal detention or public surveillance, and shall also be fined not less than 20, 000 yuan but not more than 200, 000 yuan. If the amount involved is relatively large or there are other serious circumstances, he shall be sentenced to fixed-term imprisonment of not less than three years but not more than 10 years and shall also be fined not less than 50, 000 yuan but not more than 500, 000 yuan. If the amount is huge or there are other special features, and the circumstances are not serious, he shall be sentenced to fixed-term imprisonment of not less than 10 years or life imprisonment, and shall also be fined not less than 50, 000 yuan but not more than 500, 000 yuan or be sentenced to confiscation of property.

If a unit commits the crime mentioned in this article, it shall be fined, and the persons who are directly in charge and the other persons who are directly responsible for the crime shall be sentenced to fixed-term imprisonment of not more than three years, criminal detention or public surveillance. If the amount involved is relatively large or there are other serious circumstances, they shall be sentenced to fixed-term imprisonment of not less than three years but not more than 10 years. If the amount involved is huge or there are other especially serious circumstances, they shall be sentenced to fixed-term imprisonment of not less than 10 years or life imprisonment punishment. "

Article 209 of *the Criminal Law* stipulates: "Anyone who forges, makes without authorization or sells other invoices that can be used to defraud export tax rebates or offset taxes shall be sentenced to fixed-term imprisonment of not more than three years, criminal detention or public surveillance, and shall also be fined not less than 20, 000 yuan but not more than 200, 000 yuan. If the amount involved is huge, he or she shall be sentenced to fixed-term imprisonment of not less than three years but not more than seven years and shall also be fined not less than 50, 000 yuan but not more than 500, 000 yuan. If the amount is especially huge, he or she shall be sentenced to fixed-term imprisonment of not less than seven years and shall also be fined not less than 50, 000 yuan but not more than 500, 000 yuan or be sentenced to confiscation of property.

Whoever forges, manufactures or sells invoices other than those mentioned in the preceding paragraph shall be sentenced to fixed-term imprisonment of not more than two years, criminal detention or public surveillance and shall also, or shall only, be fined not less than 10, 000 yuan but not more than 50, 000 yuan. If the circumstances are serious, he or she shall be sentenced to fixed-term imprisonment of not less than two years but not more than seven years and shall also be fined not less than 50, 000 yuan but not more than 500, 000 yuan. "

Those who illegally print, lend, resell, alter or forge tax payment certificates shall be ordered by the tax authorities to make corrections and shall be fined not less than 2, 000 yuan but not more than 10, 000 yuan. If the circumstances are serious, a fine of not less than 10, 000 yuan but not more than 50, 000 yuan shall be imposed. If a crime is constituted, criminal responsibility shall be investigated according to law.

9.6   Tax Payment Guarantee and Mortgage

Tax payment guarantee refers to the behavior that the taxpayer or other natural person, legal person or economic organization provides guarantee for the tax payable and overdue fine by way of guaranteeing, mortgaging and pledging with the approval or confirmation of tax authorities.

9.6.1   Tax Guarantee

A tax payment guarantee refers to a guarantee given by a tax payment guarantor to the tax authorities. When a taxpayer fails to pay the tax and overdue fine in accordance with the provisions of tax laws, administrative regulations or the time limit determined by the tax authorities, the tax payment guarantor shall pay the tax and overdue fine in accordance with the agreement. If approved by the tax authorities, the guarantee shall be established; if not approved by the tax authorities, the guarantee shall not be established.

The scope of tax payment guarantee includes tax, overdue fine and the cost of realizing tax and overdue fine. The expenses include mortgage, pledge registration fee, pledge custody fee, and other related expenses such as custody, auction and sale of guaranteed property.

9. 6. 2   Tax Mortgage

The tax payer's property that cannot be mortgaged as a guarantee for tax payment is the property that cannot be mortgaged. If the taxpayer fails to pay the tax and overdue fine within the time limit, the tax authorities have the right to dispose of the property according to law to offset the tax and overdue fine.

The following property shall not be mortgaged: ①Land ownership. ②Land use right, except for those stipulated in the above mortgage scope. ③Educational facilities, medical and health facilities and other social public welfare facilities of public institutions, social organizations, private non enterprise units such as schools, kindergartens, hospitals and other public welfare facilities; the property other than educational facilities, medical and health facilities and other social public welfare facilities of public institutions and social organizations such as schools, kindergartens and hospitals with the purpose of public welfare can be paid as their property. The tax and overdue fine are provided as collateral. ④Property with unclear or disputed ownership and right to use. ⑤Property that has been sealed up, detained and supervised according to law. ⑥Buildings which are confirmed to be illegal and illegal according to legal procedures. ⑦Property prohibited from circulation or non-transferable as stipulated by laws and administrative regulations. ⑧Other properties that are not mortgaged as confirmed by the tax authorities of cities or autonomous prefectures divided into districts.

9. 6. 3   Tax Pledge

Tax pledge means that the taxpayer or tax guarantor transfers his chattel or title certificate to the tax authority for possession with the consent of the tax authority, and takes the chattel or title certificate as the guarantee of tax and overdue fine. If the taxpayer fails to pay the tax and overdue fine within the time limit, the tax authorities have the right to dispose of

the chattel or certificate of title according to law to offset the tax and overdue fine. Tax pledge is divided into chattel pledge and right pledge.

Chattel pledge includes the pledge of cash and other property other than real estate. The pledge of rights includes the pledge provided by bill of exchange, check, promissory note, bond and deposit certificate.

9.7　Administration of Tax Credit

Tax credit management refers to the collection, evaluation, determination, release and application of taxpayer's tax credit information by tax authorities.

Tax credit evaluation cycle is a tax year.

There are five levels of tax credit: A, B, M, C and D.

(1) A-level tax credit is more than 90 points in the annual evaluation index.

(2) B-level tax credit is the annual evaluation index score more than 70 points but less than 90 points.

(3) The following enterprises without dishonesty listed in Item 5 above shall be subject to M-level tax credit: ①Newly established enterprises. ②Enterprises with no production and operation income in the evaluation year and the annual evaluation index score is more than 70 points.

(4) C-level tax credit is the annual evaluation index score of more than 40 points but less than 70 points.

(5) D-level tax credit is defined as the annual evaluation index score less than 40 points or determined by direct grading.

9.8　Measures for the Administration of Reporting Tax Violations

The purpose of formulating the administrative measures for reporting illegal tax acts is to protect the right of units and individuals to report taxpayers and withholding agents violating tax laws and administrative regulations and standardize the order of reporting.

The term "accusation" refers to the act of units and individuals providing clues to the tax authorities of illegal tax behaviors of taxpayers and withholding agents in the form of letters, telephones, faxes, networks and visits.

The informant may report in real name or anonymously.

The term "illegal tax act" refers to suspected tax evasion (evasion of tax payment), evasion of overdue tax payment, tax fraud, false, forged or altered invoices, and other tax related illegal acts related to tax evasion.

Protection of rights:

(1) If the informant is unwilling to provide personal information or is unwilling to disclose the behavior, the tax authorities shall respect and keep it confidential.

(2) Tax authorities should protect the legitimate rights and interests of the informant and the accused within the scope of their duties.

(3) If the staff of tax authorities have a direct interest in the matter to be reported or the informant or the accused, they shall withdraw.